WHAT IS LIFE WORTH?

*The Unprecedented Effort
to Compensate the Victims of 9/11*

■

KENNETH R. FEINBERG

PublicAffai

New York

D1113444

Book design by Mark McGarry
Set in Sabon

Library of Congress Cataloging-in-Publication Data
Feinberg, Kenneth R.
    What is life worth?: the unprecedented effort to compensate the victims of
9/11 / Kenneth R. Feinberg.
    p. cm.
Includes index.
ISBN 1-58648-323-4
    1. Reparation (Criminal justice)—United States—History. 2. Terrorism
victims' families—Legal status, laws, etc.—United States—History. 3. September 11 Terrorist Attacks, 2001. I. Title.
    KF1328.F45 2005
    362.88—dc22

                                                                    2005047699

ISBN-10 1-58648-323-4 (hc.)
ISBN-13 978-1-58648-323-4 (hc.)
ISBN-10 1-58648-451-6 (pbk.)
ISBN-13 978-1-58648-451-4 (pbk.)

FIRST PAPERBACK EDITION
10 9 8 7 6 5 4 3 2 1

*Dedicated, with respect and admiration,
to the victims, families, and all those who
suffered losses in the attacks of September 11, 2001.
Their example of faith and fortitude has inspired
millions here in America and around the world.*

Contents

Preface

Serving as the special master in charge of the 9/11 Victim Compensation Fund was a remarkable experience for me, both professionally and personally. As a lawyer and mediator, I found it to be the greatest challenge of my career, requiring me to exercise my talents, knowledge, and judgment to the fullest. At the same time, it forced me to draw deeply on the wellsprings of my capacity for empathy, compassion, strength, and wisdom, especially in dealing with grieving families who lost loved ones on September 11, 2001, and with physically injured victims whose lives were changed forever on that unforgettable day.

This book is not a diary of my experiences in relating to the 9/11 families, although personal stories are interspersed throughout the text. Instead, this book focuses on how my administration of the 9/11 fund changed me, the public policy implications of the story, and, perhaps most important, the lessons that the families can teach us about life, death, and coping with grief.

I encountered a mosaic of human emotions as I administered the 9/11 fund, a range more vast and complex than I could ever have imagined—anger and frustration tempered by love and faith; bravery and sacrifice undercut by selfishness and greed; the power of hope challenged by the shadow of despair.

Day after day, I encountered these and other emotions as I met with the families privately to discuss their loss, as well as how they planned to go forward with their lives. In this sense, the book opens a window into the surviving families' collective memory of 9/11. It also offers the public a better understanding of the personal obstacles survivors still confront in reordering their lives in the wake of 9/11.

This book also addresses crucial questions posed by the statute that created the 9/11 fund and my administration of it. This needs to be done because of the possibility—some would say inevitability—of subsequent terrorist attacks somewhere in America. How should Congress respond the next time? Did the Victim Compensation Fund constitute sound public policy? Is it a good idea that deserves to be extended into other areas?

The book also describes my administration of the fund, detailing how my support team and I determined compensation in individual cases. What factors influenced my decision making? How did I attempt to minimize the emotion and divisiveness triggered by not only the 9/11 tragedies but also a statute that categorized eligible claimants according to their economic standing? How did I try to balance the claim of the fireman's widow against the stockbroker's children or the parents of an undocumented immigrant worker? What about the claims of fiancées, same-sex partners, domestic partners, ex-spouses, infant children, estranged brothers and sisters—all competing for their share of the fund?

Focusing only on dollars in drafting the law, Congress never considered who should be authorized to speak on behalf of the dead and receive the check. In the ensuing battles between a victim's fiancée and his biological parents, between the same-sex partner and the siblings of a lost brother or sister, my legal training had little direct value.

This book also describes the impact that administering the program had on me personally. After committing three years of my life to the 9/11 fund, I could not simply return to the world that existed before the attacks. That world is gone. It disappeared in the horror of that day. Placing a value on life and distributing over $7 billion in public money to 5,562 people—all under the watchful eye of the public, Congress, and the Bush administration—affected my physical health. It also triggered a reordering of my priorities, both personal and professional. If the fund played some role in influencing the future course of the 9/11 families, it also changed my life, I believe for the better.

I need to say a word about the personal stories and quotations that appear throughout these pages. In writing this book, I've been very mindful of the need to respect the privacy of all those touched by the work of the 9/11 fund, especially the families that lost loved ones in the terror attacks and those physically injured. At the same time, it would be impossible to describe the work of the fund intelligibly without recounting some of my experiences in dealing with those families and victims and allowing them to describe their feelings in their own words. Therefore, I sought permission from a few of the 9/11 families and victims to tell a little of their story, including, in some cases, quoting their testimony from hearings I conducted on behalf of the fund. Whenever a family is mentioned by name or a family member or injured victim is quoted, it is with their express written consent. I am grateful to the individuals involved for their willingness to provide this consent.

When I make a general point that would not be clarified by reference to a particular family, I describe composite cases—usually with quotations—that are representative of many 9/11 families and victims. These composite or typical cases should not be taken as referring to any identifiable persons, and any apparent similarity to a particular individual is purely coincidental.

As every first-time author discovers, writing a book is a team effort, and I'm grateful to the many individuals who have played a role in helping me capture my experiences in these pages.

This book could not have been written without the full cooperation of officials of the Department of Justice, who provided me with helpful guidance on how to comply with all federal statutes and regulations pertaining to the publication of a book dealing with the September 11th Victim Compensation Fund of 2001. A special thanks is owed Robert McCallum, the associate attorney general, and Kenneth Zwick, director, Office of Management Programs, who coordinated the overall effort, along with Peter Keisler, assistant attorney general, Civil Division, and Chad Boudreaux, former senior counsel to the deputy attorney general. I also appreciate the contribution of Department of Justice lawyers who advised me on the intricacies and complexities of the privacy laws, particularly Stuart Frisch, general counsel of the Justice Management Division; Janice Rodgers, deputy director, Departmental Ethics Office; and Richard L. Huff, co-director, Office of Information and Privacy.

Stacy Pervall at PriceWaterhouseCoopers was most cooperative in providing me all the September 11 Fund data and statistics, which are interspersed throughout the text in corroborating the success of the Fund.

A special word of thanks to my office administrator, Camille Biros, who read various drafts and provided helpful suggestions. Camille helped administer the fund from its inception and her valuable insights, based on first-hand experience, kept me on a steady course.

I also acknowledge the valuable assistance of two loyal and dedicated secretaries, Danita Wilkins and Joyce Debass Wilkins, who typed the entire manuscript and made appropriate suggestions when clarifications were needed.

My editors at PublicAffairs offered valuable, constructive editing suggestions to a first-time author unfamiliar with the unique world of publishing. A special thank you to Kate Darnton, Lindsay Jones, and Karl Weber, who took a rough manuscript and turned it into a finished product worthy of publication.

I also thank my wife, Dede, and brother, David, for their devotion in reading my various drafts and providing me keen insight and wise counsel. The two of them were valuable resources, especially in reviewing those sections of the book dealing with my childhood and career path prior to being appointed special master of the fund.

Finally, I must express my deep thanks and gratitude to all the September 11 families and injured victims who granted permission to quote from their various 9/11 hearings and meetings with me. Over sixty family members authorized my use of their words. My effort in this book to focus on the lessons learned from meeting with these 9/11 families and victims could never have occurred without their cooperation and support. I am in their debt.

Introduction

ON SEPTEMBER 22, 2001—just eleven days after the 9/11 attacks—President George W. Bush signed into law the Air Transportation Safety and System Stabilization Act, which created the September 11th Victim Compensation Fund of 2001. This statute was like no other in American history. Drafted in haste, without due consideration of consequences and with little congressional debate, it provided generous tax-free compensation to the families of those who died on 9/11, as well as to those who were physically injured while escaping from the World Trade Center and the Pentagon. The new law authorized the attorney general of the United States to appoint a single person, with the imposing legal title of special master, to administer the 9/11 fund. Congress delegated almost unfettered discretion to this single individual to ensure the success of the program.

On November 26, 2001, I was appointed special master of the fund. I would be the point man, the visible symbol of an unprecedented law. Never before had a government offered individuals millions of dollars in tax-free compensation for a tragic loss. And never before had government funds been so unregulated. There was no earmarked congressional appropriation limiting the size of awards or constraining my discretion. My budget was unlimited; the payouts would be determined only by my personal judgment and experience.

I alone bore responsibility for fashioning the rules and regulations governing the administration of the law. And I alone served as judge and jury in deciding appropriate compensation in individual cases. But I didn't foresee that these unprecedented responsibilities would make me the target of the anger and frustration felt by the 9/11 families. Thus began the most harrowing experience of my professional life. In the end, it was also the most rewarding.

The statute creating the fund was deceptively simple in its goals and aspirations but hideously complex in its implementation. Every line of the new law raised difficult questions: Who was eligible to receive compensation? How much money should be awarded? What rationale should govern the awards? There were few guidelines spelled out in the law, and history offered little help. I looked in vain for precedent. I even turned to the Bible and other books of religious learning, hoping to find a road map, possibly a pertinent biblical allegory that would point the way. Not so. Rabbis and priests expressed sym-

Why was their loss diff. from - a plane crash, an auto accident, a random drive-by shooting?

INTRODUCTION   XVII

pathy and occasionally promised me guidance. No defini-
tive answers were forthcoming.

With a clear mandate but little sense of how to implement it, I met with family after family in a respectful
effort to understand their needs, hopes, and expectations.
It would be hard to overstate the emotional turmoil of
the 9/11 families. Many were adrift, rudderless, trying to
cope with unexpected tragedy, emotionally spent. They
were in no condition to address the practical challenges
inherent in my invitation to apply for compensation. For
thirty-two months we met each other every day, face-to-
face. I listened as they struggled to express the losses they
suffered on 9/11, the arbitrary nature of life and death,
and the emptiness they now confronted.

One day out of those thirty-two months—April 29,
2003—offers a capsule image of the swirling, conflicting
emotions that coalesced around the 9/11 fund.

My first stop that sunny morning was the offices of a
distinguished New York City law firm. Cleary Gottlieb,
Steen & Hamilton is located on the thirty-ninth floor of
One Liberty Plaza, a glass-and-steel tower overlooking
Ground Zero, the cavernous pit that had once been the
site of the World Trade Center. There I met with six families from Mexico, Peru, Ecuador, the Dominican Republic, and Puerto Rico who had lost family members on
9/11. Five of the victims had been undocumented foreign
nationals employed at the World Trade Center.

The feeling was surreal—meeting with these poor,
grief-stricken, uncertain families in a posh, glass-enclosed

conference room with a full view of the mass grave site where their loved ones had perished. The discomfort I felt caused me to squirm.

With the assistance of a lawyer and a translator, the families presented their cases one by one.

First, a father explained how he and his family had traveled all the way from Peru to meet with me to discuss their dead son, Ivhan Luis, who had been a cook at a restaurant in the World Trade Center. Ivhan had just been accepted as a student at the City University of New York. Sobbing, the elderly man recounted how his other son, despondent over the death of his brother, had committed suicide fourteen months after 9/11.

Gently I asked, "Do you understand that the payment you'll receive from the fund will be based, in part, on your son's income?"

The father nodded. Ivhan Luis had earned $8,645 in 2000, and $17,337 in 2001.

Next a wife, tears streaming down her face, described the loss of her husband, Jose Gomez, the father of her three children, who had died on September 11 along with his brother. Jose had earned $28,648 in 2000.

Then a son, Luis, spoke with pride about his father, Luis Alfonso Chimbo, born and educated in Ecuador with a degree in microbiology. Luis had moved his family to New York to seek a better life. He began working as a busboy at a Rockefeller Center cafeteria and in 1997 was hired by a restaurant in the World Trade Center, where he was quickly promoted to a management position in the

Receiving Department. In 2000, his salary was $33,717. The son submitted a letter describing his loss:

Before, it was fun, exciting, and interesting. Now everything has changed. With my father here, my mom and I were very happy. Every day was different, even though we had some fights, like all families, we worked them out every time. My dad would be the person who made us understand why fighting wasn't worth anything. He said that it only led into other bad things and then soon enough everything would come down. We didn't want that to happen. I wish all this never happened, I wish that my dad was here. Even if everything else went wrong at least we would have each other and together we would get through obstacles. . . . I don't know what is wrong with me. It seems as if I don't feel anything, but inside I do. Inside I want to burst and just talk to everyone about what I'm holding in. I want to say how much pain I have and I want to say all the pressure that I have. I have to control myself (emotionally), I have to keep track with my school work, I have to keep track about what's happening in my family, I have to also keep in mind what I have to do every day. When one thing goes wrong it seems like everything else is being pulled towards the one thing because it all goes wrong. . . . Right now, this is a messed up world. I just say "Oh Well," we have to live whatever the heck life throws at us.

Last, a brother described the loss of his twenty-two-year-old brother, Martin Zempoaltecatl. Martin was born in Mexico and had been living in New York for three years when he died. Initially a dishwasher, he trained to become a cook. He served as an apprentice cook at two restaurants before being hired as an assistant chef at a restaurant in the World Trade Center.

Martin had primary responsibility for supporting his parents in Mexico. His dream was to build them a new home and, with that goal in mind, he roomed with his two brothers, who paid most of his local expenses so that Martin could send almost all of his wages home to his parents.

On September 11, the house in Mexico was half completed. His parents could not afford to finish its construction. The family hoped to use the money from the 9/11 fund to complete construction of the house in Martin's memory. His salary in 2000 had been $20,589.

All eyes turned toward me. I was deeply aware of the cultural divide that separated me from the parents and relatives sitting around the table. I attempted to convey my personal condolences for their loss but was hesitant and tentative, unsure whether my comments were appropriate. Then I tried to describe how the 9/11 fund would work. "I expect to pay each family a minimum of $250,000," I explained. I sensed their doubt, their skepticism. The magnitude of the dollars being offered! What strings were attached?

I was moved by these poor families, some visiting the United States for the first time, meekly seeking compensation to rekindle dreams that tragedy had extinguished. I tried to reassure them. There were no tricks in the law, there was no hidden agenda. The undocumented worker status of the victims was irrelevant; I promised each family around the table that they need not fear criminal sanctions or civil fines if they applied to the fund. I would do all I could to maximize the awards and treat them fairly. A few family members smiled their thanks; others simply stared and nodded, stoic and numb with grief.

I left the meeting with a heavy heart. I realized what a huge responsibility I confronted, putting price tags on lost loved ones' lives—and on survivors' aspirations.

It's just a few miles from One Liberty Plaza to the Equitable Building at 787 Seventh Avenue in midtown Manhattan, but it seemed as if I'd traveled halfway around the world. An hour earlier, I'd been meeting with poor, humble families from South America, who did not even speak English; now I was sitting across a table from officials of the financial firm of Keefe, Bruyette & Woods. Busboys and dishwashers were not the subject of discussion here but rather investment bankers who made millions of dollars each year, some of the sixty-seven Keefe, Bruyette employees killed when United Flight 175 hit Tower Two.

Just like the Latin American families, the families of the Keefe, Bruyette partners had been devastated by unspeakable tragedy. But the kind of compensation it would take to preserve their accustomed lifestyles was of a different order of magnitude.

The Keefe, Bruyette officials fired questions at me.

"Using economic loss as a criterion, some of our families ought to receive checks of ten to twenty million from the fund. Is that going to happen?"

"Will your computations reflect only base salary, or will commissions and bonuses be factored in?"

"What about gratuitous payments made by the firm shortly after September 11 to the surviving families—will they be deducted from the award?"

A sophisticated report had been specially prepared by a distinguished economist retained by Keefe, Bruyette solely for the purpose of calculating the dead partners' awards under the new law. Would I accept the economist's assumptions about future compensation growth rates at the firm? How would I treat the generous Keefe, Bruyette pension plan in calculating awards?

For nearly an hour I walked the company officials through the policies and regulations governing payouts by the Fund. As the meeting wound down, one Keefe, Bruyette partner took me aside. "You know," he observed, "a lot of our families haven't yet applied to participate in the fund."

"I know," I replied. I was concerned about that. One of my main objectives in administering the fund was to encourage full participation by all eligible families rather than have them pursue a costly, time-consuming, and emotionally wrenching remedy through the courts.

"They're having great difficulty dealing with the financial uncertainty generated by the fund. It would help if you could give these families some indication of the size of their awards."

I understood his implication. If the family of a Keefe, Bruyette partner knew it would receive, say, $5 million dollars from the fund, it might be less inclined to sue the airlines or the FAA or the Port Authority in hopes of a $10 million or $20 million settlement.

My mind wandered back to the meeting a few hours earlier with Luis Chimbo. All Luis had wanted was an opportunity to be heard, to meet me face-to-face, and to hand me his letter describing the impact of losing his father. Now these bankers were quizzing me on the details of their firm's pension plan.

In my mind their actions demeaned the memory of the dead. Or was that unfair? The law required that these very questions be asked. These partners were only trying to understand how I would apply an unprecedented statute. Like me, they were groping for answers. Still, I thought, what did these bankers really know about "financial uncertainty"? The families of Luis Chimbo and Martin Zempoal-tecatl were the ones who knew the real meaning of the term.

At that moment, I realized that it would be impossible to satisfy the expectations of everyone participating in the fund—rich and poor, privileged and underprivileged, bankers and busboys. I began to view the program in a new light. It was not just about money, about providing bereaved families with a cash lifeline. It was about compensating for a catastrophic emotional loss—trying to fill the hole in a family's life with money.

The statute creating the 9/11 fund was an attempt to do the impossible—to provide fair repayment for the sudden loss of a loved one and some degree of justice for that loss. But in such a case, what is "fair"? What is "just"? How can life be measured in dollars and cents? Should such a calculus even be attempted, especially in a democracy founded on belief in the dignity and respect due every individual? These are questions with no simple answers.

Michael James's wife, Gricelda, died in the World Trade Center on September 11. Gricelda placed three calls on her cell phone after the attacks. The first was to her husband, telling him that she was trapped on the seventy-ninth floor and that she loved him. The second, to her oldest son, Jacobo, indicated that she was waiting for the fire fighters to rescue her. She called Jacobo again at 10:20 A.M., a few minutes before the tower collapsed. When we met to discuss the family's claim against the 9/11 fund, Jacobo described this last frantic call:

> [My mother was] still inside and she didn't know what was going to happen to her; just tell everyone I love them because she didn't know what would happen. She said they didn't have no lights in the offices now and to take care.

In applying to the fund, Michael James explained why 9/11 compensation—however generous—could never replace the loss of his wife:

> There's no value, there's no value for Gricelda. If gold is the best we have in this world, she was gold. If there's something better than gold, she was that too.

Surely all 9/11 families would say the same about their loved ones. But as special master, my responsibility was purely financial—to wield the power of the national purse on behalf of those who suffered the ultimate loss. Yet I tried to perform my job in the spirit invoked by Michael James, never forgetting that a human life is of incalculable value, beyond what gold can measure.

CHAPTER ONE

The Experience of a Lifetime

THERE HAD NEVER been a government program quite like the 9/11 fund—nor did the legal profession train lawyers with the combination of skills, judgment, and experiences needed to administer the fund. Being named special master of the 9/11 fund was the single most difficult challenge I had ever confronted in my thirty years as a lawyer. Although I pray that no one will ever have to play such a role again, the appointment was the natural culmination of my professional career.

In the early 1960s, I was an average student at rough-and-tumble Brockton High School in Brockton, Massachusetts, where my dad owned a tire store. Brockton is a blue-collar "shoe city" a few miles south of Boston, whose most distinguished citizens were boxing champions Rocky Marciano and "Marvelous" Marvin Hagler. I'll always be a Brockton boy, something that's obvious as soon as I open my mouth and speak with an unmistakable Massachusetts accent.

I joined many of my high school buddies at the University of Massachusetts, where I became fascinated by American history. Somewhat to my surprise, I turned into a first-rate student. I graduated with honors and was selected to deliver the first student commencement address at graduation. After my speech, Governor John Volpe leaned over and whispered to me, "Ken, you just said everything that I was about to say. What should I do now?" Stealing the thunder of a nationally known politician was quite a thrill for me.

I had trouble deciding on my next move. At UMass, I'd fallen in love with the stage. I played the Duke of Venice in Shakespeare's *Othello*, a servant/slave in *The Twin Menechmae*, a comedy by Plautus, and the husband in Edward Albee's seriocomic *Zoo Story*. I enjoyed the camaraderie that develops among actors during the long haul from the first reading of the script to the finished production, and I relished the laughter and applause that reward a zestful performance. So I was tempted by the idea of an acting career. But my dad stepped in with homespun—and typically wise—advice.

"Ken, most actors end up waiting tables in New York City and starving. Why not take your acting talents to law school? You can play Hamlet in front of juries."

Smart man. I attended New York University Law School, where I found myself fascinated with the law—its analytic rigor, its vital connection to social and political issues. I became an editor of the *Law Review* and graduated near the top of my class. I was selected as a law clerk by the chief judge of the State of New York, Stanley H. Fuld, one of the nation's foremost state court jurists.

I found my two years as a clerk daunting and exhilarating. Fuld's quiet demeanor masked a rigorous intellectual honesty. As his law clerk, I would prepare draft after draft of an opinion—often a dozen or more—before he was satisfied with the legal reasoning and the use of language. Only then would the opinion be ready for public release. He taught me that there is no substitute for hard work and legal craftsmanship.

Fuld derided sloppiness and shortcuts. In a moment of anger over a bit of subpar work from me, he once declared, "Now I know why I've never hired an NYU law clerk before." Coming from Judge Fuld, this was devastating, but the next day was a new day and he didn't dwell on my shortcomings. Another time he asked me to deliver a draft opinion to the state capital at Albany. After a long bus ride, I phoned him with bad news. "I'm in Albany, and my suitcase with all my clothes has just been stolen." Judge Fuld responded, "Never mind your clothes—what about the opinion?" Fortunately he had another copy in his office.

Judge Fuld died in 2004 at ninety-nine years of age. Many of us still miss him. My determination to validate Chief Judge Fuld's trust in me fueled my ambition and became a motivating factor in my professional and personal life.

The law clerks who worked for Stanley Fuld over the years make up a Who's Who of the New York bar. Perhaps the most distinguished is Jack B. Weinstein, a noted professor of evidence and civil procedure at Columbia Law School appointed to the federal bench by President Lyndon B. Johnson. A towering figure in the law, Weinstein crafted opinions that changed the legal landscape in areas as diverse as criminal law, civil procedure, race discrimination, and class actions.

Weinstein and other Fuld alumni attended annual reunions to reminisce about their days as law clerks and pay homage to their former boss. I remember my sense of awe when I began attending those gatherings. I wondered whether I, like Weinstein, would ever leave my own mark on the law or make an impact on society.

After completing a clerkship, most young lawyers would choose a position at a major law firm, perhaps on Wall Street. But I wasn't attracted to this path. I'd heard that, in a large firm, the young lawyers toil in relative anonymity and drudgery, earning good money but enjoying little opportunity to shine in the courtroom or develop their creative talents. So I opted to remain in the public arena.

I spent the next three years as a federal prosecutor in the distinguished U.S. Attorney's office in Manhattan. Here I put my acting talents to good use, litigating in dozens of criminal trials involving bank robbery, securities fraud, income tax evasion, and drug trafficking.

One of my first court appearances was as a junior assistant during the corruption trial of former Attorney General John Mitchell. The criminal allegations were unrelated to Watergate and Mitchell was acquitted, but the trial taught me valuable lessons. Watching from my seat at the prosecutor's table, I thought that the defense lawyers beat us to the punch in making certain points and arguments. I realized that there is no substitute for preparation—you have to anticipate every possible scenario. I also concluded that I would have been right about the different strategies I would have followed during that trial, which suggested to me that my courtroom instincts were sound.

I applied these dual lessons to my later work, including my role with the 9/11 fund: totally prepare yourself and then, in the heat of battle, follow your instincts.

Although most federal prosecutors in Manhattan remain in the office for five years or longer, I moved on after three, when a new challenge presented itself. In 1975, Senator Edward Kennedy was seeking a new junior counsel to assist him in his work as a member of the Senate Judiciary Committee. I had always admired Senator Kennedy—I had, after all, been a teenager in Massachusetts during the halcyon days of President John F. Kennedy and Camelot. A friend of mine knew David Burke, Kennedy's former chief of staff, who went on to become president of CBS News. Through my friend, I arranged for Burke to watch me in the courtroom. He sent word back to me that I should apply for the job.

To my delight, I was invited to Washington for an interview with Kennedy.

Wanting to be perfectly honest, I said to Senator

Kennedy, "I'm a big admirer of yours, Senator. But when it comes to the criminal law, we have some differences. I'm a prosecutor, remember."

He said, "That's all right. I'm a former prosecutor myself. I'll make the policy decisions. I'm looking for someone who's smart and creative." The senator was seeking someone who would challenge him on the issues and provide him wise counsel and independent thinking.

I was offered the job and immediately accepted—in fact, I broke the news about it to my new bride, Diane, on our honeymoon. Fortunately for me, Dede (as she's known) is extremely flexible. She loved the Washington, D.C., area, where we have lived ever since.

My five years working with Senator Kennedy were hard and immensely rewarding. I immersed myself in scores of public policy issues and debates, from criminal law reform to immigration reform, from modifications in the law governing criminal sentencing and parole, to changes in federal bail practices and the law of evidence. I worked closely with other senators and their staffs, particularly Republican Senator Orrin Hatch of Utah, who proved a valuable ally of Senator Kennedy in promoting bipartisan legislative consensus on a number of issues.

I never thought I would have such an exciting job. I loved drafting legislation, knowing that I was having an impact on society and trying to accomplish things for the public good. I was working with Kennedy at the fulcrum of power, meeting presidents and prime ministers and kings. Even his adversaries admit that Kennedy is a fabulous person. He is without a doubt the most respected senator in the U.S. Senate because he gets the most done—a true legislator. He is a hard, indefatigable worker, and, after more than forty years in the Senate, is second to none in his mastery of the legislative process.

I also became a frequent visitor at the Justice Department during the last year of the Ford administration. Together with Attorney General Edward Levi and a young counsel named Antonin Scalia, we drafted a new law governing the collection of foreign intelligence information here in the United States. The Foreign Intelligence Surveillance Act, my first foray into the mysterious world of collecting intelligence data, became one of my proudest achievements. The new law, introduced by Senator Kennedy with the support of Senator Hatch and others in the Senate and House, created a secret federal court and judicial warrant procedure for the collection of domestic intelligence information. By delineating turf it clarified as intelligence gathering the administration became more willing to take the steps necessary to gather intelligence because it had the blessing of a court.

This law served the nation well until the 9/11 terrorist attacks demonstrated that modifications were necessary to encourage better coordination between the FBI, CIA, and National Security Agency. A law drafted with the Cold War in mind needed to be rethought in the twenty-first century to take into account the changing political climate brought about by international terrorism rather than the Soviet threat.

Irritating

Under Senator Kennedy, I first served as special counsel to the Judiciary Committee then became his chief of staff. There were as many as eighty people working for Kennedy in his various offices in Washington and back in Massachusetts—a typical congressional staff. But I didn't like being chief of staff. I found that managing and scheduling were not as much fun as doing.

Senator Kennedy's unsuccessful 1980 presidential campaign marked a turning point for me. Mulling my future, I decided it was time for me to finally enter private practice. I had a wife and small children, and considerations of financial security had become a priority. I talked to various firms in Boston and New York before signing on with the distinguished firm of Kaye, Scholer Fierman Hays & Handler, which was searching for someone to start a Washington, D.C., office to handle lobbying, local litigation, and regulatory work with agencies such as the EPA, SEC, and others. It was a good time for me to make such a move. With President Ronald Reagan heading a Republican administration, public service would yield to private practice.

My job with Kaye Scholer meant I was in court occasionally; otherwise I was dealing with government contacts and doing other kinds of client work. Over the next twelve years I became a leading member of the firm, serving on the executive committee and the compensation committee. The office expanded during the early years of the Reagan administration and I was called on by various Fortune 500 companies to provide strategic advice and counsel. Things were going well. Excellent compensation allowed my wife and me to purchase a new family home. We took frequent family vacations. I had become a successful "Washington lawyer" and looked forward to decades of success in the private sector. Still, I felt restless.

All this changed in the mid–1980s because of Jack Weinstein, the distinguished Fuld alum. My lingering love of the stage had brought us together. I played the part of Chief Judge Fuld in a skit during a roast at the 1971 reunion of Fuld clerks, and my comic rendition of Fuld's personal mannerisms brought down the house—and elicited tears of laughter from Weinstein. We also shared a Kennedy connection—Jack's nomination to the bench by President Johnson had been at the instigation of Robert F. Kennedy, my old boss's brother. The two of us became fast friends.

By 1984 Weinstein was a federal district judge in Brooklyn, New York. He was handling the Agent Orange litigation brought by thousands of Vietnam veterans claiming injuries due to exposure to the herbicide in Southeast Asia. He called on me to assist in efforts to settle the case.

Dow, Monsanto, and several other chemical companies that had been involved with manufacturing dioxin for use as a herbicide in Vietnam were the defendants. In the form of Agent Orange, dioxin had allegedly injured Vietnam vets who started suing in the 1970s. For six years, thousands of Agent Orange cases wound their way through the courts before the federal judiciary ordered all the cases sent to Weinstein for resolution—they knew he wouldn't let them drag on indefinitely.

Weinstein got the cases in 1983 and consolidated them into one class action. This was common in consumer fraud, securities fraud, and commercial disputes, but extending it to a tort (a civil wrong) was new. It was a good thing; consolidating the cases greatly increased efficiency, so victims wouldn't have to wait for years for a resolution.

Agent Orange initiated the modern era of mass torts and was the biggest such case up to that time. Today it pales by comparison with cases such as the Dalkon Shield ($2.5 billion in total liability), tobacco (potentially up to $250 billion), DES, heart valves, and asbestos.

In February 1984—just two months before the case was due to go to trial—Weinstein informed me that he wanted to appoint me as special master with a mandate to help the parties settle the dispute. (Special master is a judicial term from the common law. It usually refers to a judicial officer appointed to assist a court in some way.)

"Ken," he said, "The trial will be very problematic and time consuming. It would be a good thing to settle this case. Do your best." I promised to try.

And thus I began my new career as a mediator. My formal qualifications were nonexistent; I had no prior experience as a mediator and had not even taken a mediation course during law school. But Weinstein concluded that I was the right man for the job. He trusted my judgment as a fellow Fuld clerk in good standing. In addition, my years with Senator Kennedy convinced Weinstein that

I had the political skills to help the parties reach a settlement. I also possessed the determination, flexibility, and creativity to solve the legal problems dividing the litigants. These qualities would compensate for whatever formal mediation training I lacked.

I would have to learn by doing. I began meeting with lawyers, Vietnam veterans, and representatives of the defendant chemical companies. I started by asking the chemical companies, "How much are you willing to pay to get rid of this entire class action?" They answered, A *total* of $25,000. Then I asked the plaintiffs, "How much are you willing to take to settle?" Their answer: $1.25 billion. "Okay, we're making progress," I said. "Now let's see if we can narrow that gap."

I spent the next six weeks working with the two sides seven days a week, threatening, cajoling, explaining, enticing, promising. The trial was coming up and both sides were uncertain about their prospects—that was key. You have to take advantage of uncertainty in the law. I talked with Judge Weinstein once or twice a day. I read all the briefs and read about the science. I told the plaintiffs they'd be unlikely to be able to show causation; I warned the defendants about the dangers of Brooklyn juries, which were notoriously generous to plaintiffs, and I reminded them about what would happen to their companies' stock prices as a trial dragged on. And I emphasized the fact that they had insurance that would pay the settlement. (Some litigation was needed to make the insurance companies pay.)

The keys to forging a settlement were empathy (let them vent), doggedness, preparation, creativity, and flexibility. For example, after we agreed on an overall settlement amount—$180 million—we had to come up with a formula to allocate the cost among the various chemical companies. Should we use the relative market shares of the different companies as the criterion? But one company could claim that its product contained less dioxin, which meant less disease-producing potential. What about the length of time each company had produced the chemical? But that might not correlate with actual usage of the product. In the end, a combination of three factors was devised—volume, qualitative ingredients, and time—which seemed the fairest way to allocate responsibility.

Then there was the issue of who gets the money. The plaintiffs couldn't prove that any individual Vietnam veteran's disease was caused by Agent Orange, so we agreed to compensate whoever was most seriously injured regardless of a causal connection to dioxin.

On one of the last days before trial, Judge Weinstein brought in both sides after I'd reported optimistically to him. He offered them a tray of prune Danish—"to get them moving," as he wryly noted. After six weeks of mediation we were able to announce a settlement—one day before the jury was scheduled to be impaneled. Neither side was completely happy, which of course means it was a good settlement. Unfortunately 80 percent of the litigants got nothing, since there was not enough money. A totally disabled vet received around $20,000. The court ordered the money put into the bank and paid out over ten years. Thanks to the interest accrued, the initial settlement sum of $180 million turned into a payout of approximately $300 million.

By today's standards, of course, the settlement was modest. And the amounts received by the injured vets fell far short of what it would have taken to fully compensate them for their losses. Still, it was a better deal than they would have likely received from the courts, and on that basis I consider it a good piece of mediation work.

The settlement was front-page news in every major newspaper. It brought an end to a thorny, emotional litigation that had dragged on in the courts for over six years.

It also brought an end to my professional career as a litigator. The settlement was viewed favorably by business—the idea that mediation could short-circuit problems morphed into the idea that a third-party magician can help us bridge our differences. Fortune 500 companies suddenly wanted me to settle everything.

My life changed overnight. At the time, there were almost no other well-known mediators, except in the somewhat specialized world of labor–management disputes. In effect, I helped create a whole new area of practice. For the next eight years at Kaye Scholer I did more and more mediation. I helped resolve many mass injury claims and complex litigations. I became a settlement guru who negotiated claims involving such varied products as asbestos, Dalkon Shield, heart valves, and breast implants. Once settlements were achieved, I developed formulas for the distribution of settlement proceeds, often involving hundreds of millions of dollars, and allocated these proceeds to eligible claimants.

I loved this work because when you are mediating or negotiating, you're in the driver's seat. I also loved the diversity of the workload, which involved a continually changing cast of personalities and a wide-ranging array of cases. By 1992 I launched my own firm devoted exclusively to resolution of complex disputes. I called it Kenneth R. Feinberg and Associates. We focused on mass torts and such other fields as commercial, environmental, insurance, securities, and intellectual property law.

Our clients were almost always Fortune 500 companies, and the plaintiffs included victims of asbestos, the Dalkon Shield, securities fraud, environmental exposure, and commercial wrongdoing. I usually got involved when both sides had a trial date looming. Either one or both sides would come to me, or sometimes a judge asked me to get involved. Judge Weinstein, who had launched me on this new career, continued to call on me; for example, he brought me in on the Shoreham nuclear plant closing case, as well as the asbestos and DES cases in Manhattan.

Consequently my national reputation as a mediator and settlement administrator was well established when the 9/11 terrorist attacks changed our world irrevocably.

On that unforgettable morning, I was at the University of Pennsylvania law school teaching a class on mass torts.

I walked out of class and found the students congregated around a TV in the lobby of the law school building. Only one tower had been hit at that point, so everyone was assuming that this was simply an innocent mishap, caused, most likely, by the unskilled pilot of a small plane.

I ran down to 30th Street Station and caught the train to Washington, D.C. Before reaching the next stop (Wilmington) I learned that a second plane had hit the other tower via scuttlebutt from people with radios. At Wilmington, everybody was in shock—the Pentagon had also been hit.

By this time, the train service had shut down. Some lawyer friends of mine got off with me; we hired a taxi and drove to D.C.

Our youngest son Andrew was at Middlebury College so we were weren't worried about him. Our oldest son, Michael, however, was a law student at NYU. And my daughter Leslie was an undergraduate student at Georgetown, just across the Potomac from the Pentagon. My wife and I were beside ourselves about Michael and Leslie. After an hour or so they both contacted us and reassured us that they were all right.

In the ensuing weeks, I realized that I didn't personally know anyone who was injured or killed on 9/11. (Now I know thousands! And I'm sure that if I bump into one of these families thirty years from now I will remember them.)

In the immediate aftermath of the attacks, I was like any other American citizen: shocked and dismayed by the

destruction and loss of life; enraged at the terrorists for
their brazen disregard of human decency; and filled with
a surge of patriotism and a desire to do whatever I could
to help support our nation in this time of trial. Although
I had no personal connection to the tragedy, like many
Americans I experienced a sense of frustration and helplessness. Then, I came across a newspaper article a week
or so after the attacks, describing the idea of a 9/11 compensation fund. That's what got me interested in a program that would engage my intellect, energies, and
emotions for the better part of three years.

The 9/11 fund was a congressional afterthought.

Immediately after September 11, the airlines ran to
Congress for help, maintaining that without federal loan
guarantees and other relief, they would go bankrupt. Passengers were afraid to fly; airports were shut down.
Unless Congress moved fast, there would be thousands of
lawsuits targeting the airlines, the World Trade Center,
and any other companies connected to 9/11. Federal help
was the only way out, and Congress came to the rescue.
It decided that the airline industry must remain finan-
cially secure; that airline bankruptcies were contrary to
the national interest; and that the terrorists would not
succeed in bringing America's transportation industry to
its knees. Planes must continue to fly. The airlines and
their lobbyists worked overtime, knocking on Senate and
House doors seeking government protection. Their pleas

did not fall on deaf ears. Concerned about a possible national transportation emergency, Congress came to the airlines' rescue. A law would be passed to prop up the beleaguered industry.

But patriotism played a role as well. The 9/11 terrorists had attempted to deliver a knockout blow to the American people. Staggered but still standing, how would America respond? One way was to send a signal to the world that the murderers would not achieve their long-term objective of paralyzing American society. "Business as usual" became the mantra; societal disruption must be kept to a minimum. The Air Transportation Safety and System Stabilization Act was a patriotic response to 9/11. It demonstrated the unity of the American people, the cohesiveness of the nation. We would get through this together.

Airline executives were concerned about litigation— thousands of sympathetic 9/11 victims and their families rushing to court, heart-wrenching pleas of trial lawyers blaming them for failing to safeguard innocent Americans against the murderous terrorist attacks. But it was not the fear of multimillion-dollar jury verdicts that drove the airlines to seek congressional assistance. Airline officials were confident that they would ultimately prevail in court. But that could take years. In the meantime, the likelihood of thousands of lawsuits would cast a liability shadow over the airline industry for a decade or more. Such uncertainty would deflate airline stocks. It would also remind the traveling public about the risks of airline travel. Loan guarantees were not enough. The airlines needed help from Congress to stay out of court.

And so Congress quickly enacted the new law. It provided loan guarantees and other financial protections designed to keep the airlines in business. It also discouraged lawsuits. Although it did not prohibit litigation, the new statute limited the financial liability of the airlines in the event of a successful lawsuit. It also required that those 9/11 families determined to sue the airlines could do so, but only in federal court in New York City, not in their hometowns before sympathetic judges and juries. Families who lost loved ones at the Pentagon or in Shanksville, Pennsylvania, where UA Flight 93 crashed, would now have to travel to New York to pursue their lawsuits. Other families from as far away as California, the home of many of the airline passengers on AA Flight 11 and UA Flight 175, which crashed into the World Trade Center, would similarly find the prospect of traveling to New York a daunting reason not to bring a lawsuit.

More important, the new law placed a cap on the financial liability of the airlines and World Trade Center. If the expense of coming to New York did not pose barriers to lawsuits, restrictions on financial recoveries most certainly would. Even if some 9/11 families were determined to sue, a cap on recovery would discourage the trial lawyers from accepting the challenge. Congress limited the airlines' financial exposure to $6 billion, $1.5 billion in insurance available for each of the four planes hijacked by the terrorists. World Trade Center liability was also capped. All personal injury and death claims, property damage claims, business interruption claims—claims of any type—would be subject to this insurance limitation.

Since these limited funds were obviously inadequate to pay for all property, injury, and death claims arising out of 9/11, the new law dramatically discouraged lawsuits. Why would the family of a 9/11 victim face the uncertainty of a lawsuit far from home, litigate for years, and, even if fortunate enough to prevail, only recover two cents on the dollar because of the limited pot made available by the statute? This was a risk few families would be willing to undertake. Add to this the cost of such lawsuits, the likelihood of airline appeals tying up the courts for years, and the fact that 30–40 percent of any proceeds would be paid straight to the family's attorney—suddenly, suing the airlines didn't appear so attractive. In short, the new statute accomplished its objective: it discouraged trial lawyers and their clients from seeking 9/11 redress in the courts.

But if 9/11 lawsuits were discouraged, what other effective remedy would be made available to 9/11 victims and their families? If access to the courts was not a viable option, if airline liability ran counter to the national interest, would Congress offer an alternative in its place? The trial lawyers, particularly the Association of Trial Lawyers of America and its respected president, Leo Boyle, posed this question to the Congress. If the traditional lawsuit route was not available to compensate those who might otherwise sue, shouldn't a new avenue be created by Congress? Didn't the 9/11 victims deserve a new mechanism to achieve compensation for their loss? Providing loan guarantees to a beleaguered airline industry in the wake of 9/11 could be construed as a patriotic act; restricting lawsuits and raising barriers to courtroom access could not. Congress was playing to the fears of the American people, which was downright un-American.

Arguing that it was unfair to effectively immunize the airline industry from liability while denying the victims of 9/11 an adequate legal remedy, the trial lawyers insisted that an alternative compensation mechanism be part of the new law. The trial lawyers were not interested in expending political capital by taking on the airlines in a time of national crisis. They recognized that airline litigation was a luxury the nation could not afford. But the trial lawyers and their allies in Congress also believed that some alternative compensation vehicle should be made available to 9/11 victims.

Congress debated the airline bailout bill for days, but it added the compensation program in one day as a hasty afterthought. Title IV of the new law was the result. Added to the statute at the eleventh hour, Title IV provided 9/11 victims with a voluntary alternative to lawsuits. With Representative Richard Gephardt and Senator Charles Schumer leading the way, and with the active drafting assistance of the trial lawyers, Congress created a unique legislative program to compensate 9/11 victims.

The statute was deceptively simple. It stated that any eligible 9/11 families and victims who voluntarily decided to forgo litigation against the airlines, the World Trade Center, and others could apply to a special fund to receive compensation. And they would not have to prove airline liability to receive such compensation. Speed and efficiency would replace finger pointing in the courtroom. Those eligible were offered a unique statutory choice: sue in court or participate in the fund, one or the other. Individual victims and family members could choose the swifter, more certain route of applying to the fund or could file a lawsuit of uncertain merit and litigate for years in the hope of winning a pot of gold in the litigation lottery. They would have to make their choice by December 22, 2003, which was the deadline for filing an application to participate in the fund.

In the months and years ahead, I would often ask myself whether Congress fully appreciated the implications of creating such a generous no-fault compensation program. I don't think Congress understood the dilemma of providing compensation only to a narrowly defined group of individual claimants. Was that really fair? How would I explain to Oklahoma City families why they were ineligible for compensation? Only 9/11 victims would receive compensation—not the victims of other terrorist attacks such as Oklahoma City, the African embassy bombings in Kenya, the sailors killed on the USS *Cole,* anthrax victims, and even those killed or injured in the first World Trade Center attack in 1993. Compensation was targeted only to those who suffered tragedy on 9/11. The congressional rush to enact the new statute in the wake of 9/11 left many open questions. I would become the point man to fill in the blanks.

A drumbeat of criticism was directed at the statute from the very beginning. Some critics maintained that the compensation program was merely added to the statute at the last moment, that the real objective of Congress was to bail out the airlines to make sure they avoided bankruptcy. (That was true.) Others asserted that this unique public compensation program should have received more intense congressional consideration, weighing the pros and cons of establishing such a fund for a narrowly defined group of individuals. (Also true.) Still others argued that, at a time of mushrooming deficits in a post–9/11 economy, Congress should not be in the business of creating an additional entitlement program. (Arguable.)

Although all of these criticisms had merit, I believe the supporters of the fund had the better argument. Clearly the congressional effort was aimed primarily at protecting the airline industry, but Congress could have done so without creating a generous public compensation program. And, although Congress did act in haste, time was of the essence. In the wake of the 9/11 tragedy, Congress was compelled to do *something,* and so it tried to do it all—to save the airlines and preserve the transportation infrastructure of American society while coming to the aid of survivors in distress. I considered this compassionate.

Congress could have left the victims with no remedy except the tortured, obstacle-ridden path to the courthouse. It could also have helped the airlines and left victims with no special remedy at all. Instead, it came to the rescue. Whatever the technical flaws with the statute, whatever the motivation of the Senate and House, a public compensation program, generous and compassionate, was enacted into law. The critics can have their due. But the Fund became the law of the land—in my judgment, wisely.

The law creating the 9/11 fund became effective on September 22, 2001, less than two weeks after the attacks. When I read about the pending appointment of a special master to administer the fund, I immediately telephoned Senator Chuck Hagel of Nebraska, a friend and adviser from my Agent Orange days. Chuck had been a deputy administrator of the Veterans Administration during the settlement negotiations and was a Vietnam veteran himself. Although the federal government ultimately refused to participate in the settlement, Chuck offered valuable advice to both Weinstein and me concerning how best to approach the emotionally fragile Vietnam veterans' community. We forged a friendship that continued when Chuck returned to his home in Nebraska to run for election for the U.S. Senate.

Despite entering the race as a decided underdog, he won the election. (I pointed with pride to the fact that I was one of the earliest supporters and financial contributors to his campaign.) Now, reading about the new 9/11 statute, I contacted Chuck and asked him if, despite my strong Kennedy background, he thought I might be considered for the post by the Republican Bush administration. "Leave it to me," he said, "I know John Ashcroft from our days in the Senate and you're the best man for the job." The fact that Chuck was able to advance my candidacy with the attorney general, as well as the Republican administration of President Bush, is a tribute to his powers of persuasion.

I interviewed twice for the job, both times with Attorney General John Ashcroft. The interviews were courteous and professional. Our first meeting was devoted to sizing each other up. The attorney general inquired why I, a former chief of staff to Senator Kennedy, would want to be considered for a position in a Republican administration. I explained that millions of Americans were searching for ways to help the families and nation post–9/11. What better way for me to make a contribution than to assume the complex task of special master? It would be the culmination of my legal career specializing in resolving disputes and administering courtroom settlements.

The attorney general smiled and offered me some friendly advice. "Nothing you did before will prepare you for administering this statute," he said. We spent the rest of our time discussing the new law and trying to predict the challenges of implementing Congress' intentions. There was little precedent to guide us. The compensation program would need to be created out of whole cloth.

In our second meeting, Ashcroft explained to me that the special master would not require any Senate confirmation, that the attorney general alone had the statutory authority to select the individual. He was also frank in describing his concerns about the uncertainties of the new law. We discussed the thankless nature of the assignment and how tricky it might be to handle the confused, angry, frustrated families. We agreed that the Congress might rue the day it established a compensation program requiring different awards based on individual economic circumstances.

Ashcroft warned me that he would be relying on the wisdom and judgment of the individual selected to administer the program. And once that person was selected, political realities made firing and replacing him extremely problematic. I promised that I, if selected, would work closely with the Department of Justice and the administration to implement the statute.

Then I dropped a stunner: if he appointed me, I would work without pay.

Thinking about the issue of compensation prior to the second interview, I had come to the conclusion that being paid for my work was out of the question. In a time of national emergency and grief, I thought it would be unseemly and inappropriate to seek compensation. And, like many Americans, I wanted to contribute to the relief effort in some way. Millions of Americans were donating money to 9/11 charities. Others were volunteering their time to come to the rescue of those in need. What could I do? Negotiation was my greatest talent. Here was one way I could help.

But I had another, less selfless motive in offering to work without pay. If appointed, I knew I would confront formidable obstacles in administering the new law. Here was a unique statute enacted in haste with one visible sole official granted unprecedented discretionary authority to administer it, answerable to a grief-stricken, emotional, and angry group of 9/11 families and victims. With all the criticism sure to be directed at me, I wanted to avoid additional criticism that I was receiving compensation for my work. I guessed that some families would accuse me of earning "blood money" on the backs of the dead and injured. Accepting the attorney general's assignment pro bono would preclude such criticism.

The attorney general accepted my pro bono offer with gratitude. He agreed that, if appointed, I would become a special government employee and would be permitted to remain in my law firm while administering the program.

My meeting with Mitch Daniels, director of the Office of Management and Budget (and currently governor of Indiana), also went well. He immediately impressed me as somebody who understood the statute and all the problems associated with it. He made it clear to me that the administration had agreed to the compensation fund with great reservations; it was not the cost that troubled him so much as the precedent it might set for future entitlement programs. He mused out loud about the wisdom of singling out a small segment of American society for such generous treatment. He wondered whether the statute was sound public policy. But the administration had gone along, and we discussed the mechanics of implementing the program. I left Daniels instilled with confidence that the administration was committed to the fund and would support me in administering the program. After our interview, I considered Daniels an ally.

Still, there was one unavoidable question. Why would a former chief of staff to Senator Edward Kennedy— born, raised, and schooled in a liberal bastion like Massachusetts—be selected by a Kennedy political adversary, John Ashcroft, to administer this unprecedented program? My political résumé did not exactly provide me with the blue-chip qualifications necessary to serve as the attorney general's high-profile special master. Wouldn't I pose too much political risk for the Bush administration?

In a sense, the question answered itself; the very nature of the political risk involved in the 9/11 fund gave Ashcroft every incentive to distance himself from it. If the program proved a success, the attorney general had exercised wisdom and sound judgment in making a selection based on merit rather than party affiliation or ideology. If, instead, the statute proved controversial and the fund unwieldy and unjust, the blame would land on me and my administration of the program. As Senator Hagel shrewdly put it, "The last thing you want is a buddy of the president's in that job."

In addition, it was clear to me and the attorney general that the special master would have to be someone with experience and skill in administering such a program. This was not a statute to be implemented by some former judge or member of Congress seeking part-time work in the autumn days of a public career. The job would be tough. It would entail hands-on day-to-day work meeting with families in grief. Delegation to others would be minimal. The attorney general would not be available to micromanage the program. He was far too busy with urgent issues of national security and terrorism, and would, by necessity, need to trust the expertise and good judgment of his appointee. The success of the program would depend on the special master. Experience would be crucial.

Politically and professionally, I appeared to have the right qualifications.

My appointment was announced on November 26, 2001—coincidentally, the same day that Attorney General Ashcroft hosted the Kennedy family at a reception commemorating the renaming of the Justice Department building in honor of Robert F. Kennedy. ("Quite a day for the Kennedys," he remarked to me with a grin.)

With my appointment official, Senate and House members looked to me to implement their best intentions in enacting the statute. Clearly Congress had a vested interest in the ultimate success of the fund but kept its support muted and largely behind the scenes, since how the new statute would play out in the court of public opinion remained unclear. The Senate and House would support my efforts, but outside of the public eye.

I stood alone in administering the statute. I alone would take the heat from families and public alike, and that was exactly what I was hired for.

CHAPTER TWO

Shouldering the Load

MY FIRST JOB was to pull together a competent staff to operate the fund since I anticipated claims being filed by thousands of 9/11 families and victims. I would need a large staff to process the applications and make the initial calculations, as well as a handful of skilled and loyal aides to guide me in implementing the statute.

I started with Deborah Greenspan, a lawyer in my law firm who had been at my side since my earliest days in private law practice decades earlier. More than any other single individual, she would earn the confidence and trust of the administration with her completely apolitical attitude, her careful attention to detail, and her unparalleled knowledge of every section and line of the new statute.

Jacqueline Zins, a part-time attorney at my firm, agreed to expand her role to help draft the regulations and design the program. To that duo I added Jordy Feldman, an impressive former student of mine at the University of Pennsylvania Law School who had just graduated and written me seeking "something exciting" as a first job. These three lawyers would become deputy special masters, my kitchen cabinet, and executive committee. I would rely on their input as I made major decisions.

I also needed somebody for the day-to-day administration of the program, an individual who could manage the large staff infrastructure and make sure the trains ran on time. Here I turned to my law firm administrator, Camille Biros, who had been at my side since my days with Senator Kennedy. Efficient, capable, and loyal, Camille would assume the unenviable task of overseeing the entire operation. It would be her responsibility to make sure that we functioned as one team, supporting one another, avoiding cross-purposes.

I was also extremely fortunate to receive the complete cooperation of two administration lawyers assigned to make the 9/11 fund a reality. Jay Lefkowitz, the brilliant former general counsel at OMB, had taken a leave of absence from his very successful private law practice to join the Bush administration. Jay impressed me at our very first meeting as somebody who was determined to make the program work. Whatever his political views and ideological predisposition, he proved pragmatic and cooperative. He became a trusted ally and friend.

We were joined by Phil Perry, a first-rate lawyer and acting associate attorney general at the Justice Department. Quiet but determined, Phil was the Justice Department's man at the table, the attorney general's eyes and ears. I quickly welcomed his involvement in the program. I wanted the attorney general's representative to be an inextricable part of the entire effort (thereby fulfilling my promise to Ashcroft to work closely with him), and I valued Phil's judgment and suggestions. The final regulations needed the imprimatur of the Department of Justice if bipartisanship was to be achieved. For personal, professional, and political reasons, Phil was essential. (Only later did I learn he was also Vice President Cheney's son-in-law.)

Immediately after I was appointed, Debby and I sat down with Jay, Phil, and other Department of Justice officials to draft a request for proposal, inviting interested accounting firms and consultants to bid on the job of administering the 9/11 fund. (Although I would work pro bono, along with those assisting me from my law firm, I did not and could not expect a staff of a couple of hundred people to work without compensation.) Five firms made the final cut and we awarded the Department of Justice contract to one of the largest and most distinguished accounting firms in the nation, PriceWaterhouseCoopers (PWC). It would staff the claims facility operation, renting space across the Potomac in Virginia, within a mile of the Pentagon.

The firm's mandate was extensive—to open and staff offices throughout the East Coast and California; to handle all mailings and process all applications; to make sure that claimants were eligible to receive 9/11 awards; to answer all inquiries from confused families, interested parties, and the public; and, using its technical expertise, to make the initial individual award calculations for each eligible claimant and send them on to me and my team for review and final approval. It would be an enormous undertaking and, despite the vast experience and technical know-how of PWC, I knew there would be difficult moments. We were all writing on a blank slate. Trial by error would govern our conduct.

The new law had established a vague three-part formula for computing individual awards.

First, the *economic loss* suffered by the death or physical injury of a 9/11 victim would be calculated. A concept well grounded in the law, this meant that the economic circumstances of each 9/11 victim would drive compensation paid to that victim's family. I could not imagine a more provocative provision of the new statute. It almost guaranteed that the families of a stockbroker or bond trader who died on September 11 would receive more public money than the survivors of a firefighter, soldier, or dishwasher. This provision had a clear rationale. If lawsuits were to be discouraged, a key principle underlying such lawsuits—economic loss suffered by the victim of a negligent act—should be incorporated into the alternative compensation program. It made sense as a matter of public policy. But I knew it would anger 9/11 families, who would demand to know why the life of their wife or daughter was worth less than their next door neighbor's.

Second, the statute required calculation of *noneconomic loss*, the pain and suffering of the 9/11 victim and the resulting emotional distress inflicted on surviving family members. Again, this concept was well grounded in the law of torts, a key characteristic of any lawsuit. But how could it be applied here? Did the Congress expect me to calculate different amounts of noneconomic loss in each and every case? That was impossible. I could not engage in such a claim-by-claim determination. I refused to exercise Solomonic judgment in calibrating individual degrees of pain and suffering and emotional distress. Who was I to determine whether the victim had been killed instantly when the planes hit the World Trade Center or had died a slower death from suffocation, burns, or the collapse of the Towers. Juries were required to make such distinctions in the courtroom; I would not. Not only was such a task impossible, but any attempt at it would fuel family divisiveness and discontent. I would need to figure a way to satisfy this part of the statute without alienating the very families it was meant to help.

non- econ. pain & suffering

Some members of Congress, such as Senator Don Nickels of Oklahoma, concerned about the potential runaway costs of the program and the unfortunate precedent created by the statute, were determined to put a lid on the government's obligation to compensate 9/11 victims and their families. Consequently a third requirement was added, mandating that all collateral sources of income available to a claimant—life insurance, pension payments, workers' compensation, social security death and disability payments, public victim assistance, any onetime death benefit paid to surviving families by the victim's employer—be deducted from any 9/11 award.

This statutory curve ball turned a tort-based compensation program into a type of social welfare program, a "public safety net" designed to guarantee that no 9/11 family would be made destitute by the tragedy. The government would provide tax-free compensation to those eligible, but payments would, in effect, be available as a last resort, after all other private and public sources of compensation were first considered and deducted. Only then would 9/11 compensation kick in.

Congress did not stop with this three-part formula. Acknowledging that the statute had been written hastily, without the luxury of Senate and House hearings to consider the consequences and implications of the new program, it decided to insert a safety valve. It worried that the three-part statutory formula might not work in practice. What if payments were too imbalanced? The family of a stockbroker who died in the World Trade Center, suffering a huge economic loss, might theoretically receive $30 or $40 million dollars of compensation; meanwhile, the survivors of a waiter or a dishwasher in a restaurant in the World Trade Center might be awarded, after collateral sources of income were deducted, next to nothing. Congress became gun-shy about the language of the statute and its rigid formula for sticking price tags on individual lives. There were simply too many imponderables. How would the new law work in practice? Nobody knew. Senate minority leader Tom Daschle expressed the view of

[handwritten margin note: Special Master as safety valve]

most in Congress when he asked, "Do you want to put a value on human life right now? I don't."

This was where the special master came in as a "compensation czar." He would oversee the program and exercise broad discretion in individual cases to make sure that justice was done—and unanticipated consequences were avoided. I accepted the assignment well aware of the uncertainties and inconsistencies in the statute. Both Congress and the administration were looking to me to make sure that their handiwork—drafted in haste— would prove a success. The entire effort would depend on the judgment and skill of one individual—Kenneth Feinberg—endowed with enormous power.

To understand the nature of the 9/11 fund, it's necessary to consider its context within the American system of tort law.

[handwritten margin note: Tort Law options]

Congress might have chosen to give all the families equal money. In that case, the special master's role would have been limited to determining claimant eligibility. But that flat amount would have had to be high enough to discourage lawsuits. Probably $2 million would have been enough, but Congress would never pass such a law. The most relevant precedent, the Public Safety Death Benefits Law (1971), gave a modest $250,000 to the families of peace officers killed in the line of duty. Japanese Americans who were interned during World War II received $20,000 and an apology. Giving away amounts anywhere close to $2 million would require delegating to somebody the authority to make the decisions and take the political heat.

Did Congress expect the compensation fund to make payments averaging $2 million? Frankly, I don't think they gave the dollar amount a moment's thought before passing the law. But at one point the number crunchers did estimate a total cost of $12 billion for the fund, thinking there might be more injured and dead than turned out to be the case.

With my core staff in place, we began the work of drafting the regulations that would govern the program. First we had to figure out exactly how the fund would work in practice. A 9/11 family would need to know what forms it had to complete, what submission deadlines it had to meet, what standards would be applied in evaluating each claim and, of course, the estimated size of the awards. On these issues, and many others, Congress had largely been silent. It would be up to me, exercising my largely unfettered statutory discretion, to decide how claims would be considered and awards rendered.

Time was tight. The administration and Congress had enacted the new law in record time and consequently I felt intense pressure to act swiftly. The 9/11 families were in distress and any delays in providing financial assistance would lead to charges of "too little, too late." I pushed my staff hard. We worked around the clock to draft and redraft the new regulations. I had always been an early riser, arriving at my office by 6:00 A.M. But now the stress of fashioning regulations and responding immediately to family inquiries resulted in an even longer work day. I'd arrive at my office by 5:00 A.M. and often remained until

[handwritten margin note: what KF's staff had to do]

well after 8:00 P.M. There was no time for regular meals so I would eat a sandwich at my desk or schedule a staff meeting around a working lunch.

At least once a week, I would meet with officials of PWC at meetings chaired by Debby Greenspan. Interspersed with these scheduled meetings would be hastily arranged meetings at the Justice Department with Jay, Phil, and other administration officials. These meetings at the department were critically important. Together, we would sit around a conference table and debate and resolve tough policy issues confronting the fund in a spirit of collegiality and respect. No hint of political advantage or ideology ever characterized these discussions. We were all in this together, trying to ensure ultimate success.

First we considered how much compensation should be awarded for noneconomic loss. We initially set the figure at $250,000 for the death of the victim and $50,000 for each surviving spouse and dependent, leaving room to modify these amounts if warranted by extraordinary circumstances.

how much?

There was also the volatile issue—completely ignored by the Congress—of which family members could apply to the fund and how fund awards would be distributed to the families. Who would receive the money? Could the spouse of a 9/11 victim file a claim over the objection of the victim's parents? What if the brother of the victim wanted to file but the sister objected? What about engaged persons and same-sex partners? Did they have

who could file?

any rights under the new statute? The regulations had to deal with these issues. And, since those who filed a claim waived their right to sue the airlines and the World Trade Center, this decision concerning who had the right to file and who received the award had critically important implications.

I didn't want to become embroiled in internecine warfare over the filing of claims and the distribution of fund awards. I had neither the time nor the Solomonic skill needed to referee emotional battles between and among family members. Once again, I established what I thought to be a fair solution to the problem of distribution. If the 9/11 victim had executed a will, I would follow it (within reason; as the attorney general pointed out to me in one of our private meetings, "You should not be giving public money to the Dog and Cat Museum, even if the victim said so in his will"). Unfortunately, most 9/11 victims had not executed wills. So, in cases where there was no will, the regulations made clear that the law of the state of the victim's domicile would determine who could file and who was eligible to receive the money. If a victim who died in the World Trade Center lived in New York or New Jersey or Virginia, I would look to the probate and wrongful death laws of those states.

How should we treat the claims of engaged persons and same-sex partners? Again, we decided to look to the local law of the victim's domicile and attempt to mediate a consensual resolution of the dispute.

The fund was not limited to compensating death

claims. It also addressed the concerns of those who suffered physical injuries but miraculously survived on September 11. I was surprised to find that there were few serious injury victims. All occupants of the planes were killed, and most individuals at the World Trade Center and Pentagon either escaped relatively unharmed or died. On September 11, hospitals waited for a flood of critically injured victims that never arrived. Those most seriously injured, probably no more than eighteen, suffered third-degree burns while escaping from the buildings. I decided, therefore, not to provide a presumptive range of awards in such cases but rather to evaluate each claim individually and determine an appropriate award.

The regulations recognized that economic loss in such cases would be modest; most of those injured continued to receive full salaries. But the pain and suffering of the burn victims, as well as the emotional distress visited on their families, would be substantial. The burn victims who suffered permanent disfigurement and months of hospital recuperation eventually received very generous awards, a few in excess of $8 million. These were individuals who managed to escape from the horror through a combination of luck, circumstance, determination, and, some would add, faith. Burned over 85 percent of their bodies, facing an uncertain future monopolized by daily reminders of the tragedy, they were so badly injured that no amount of compensation could prove sufficient.

The regulations also had to address the less seriously injured, particularly firefighters, police officers, and other

aftermath
effects—
Dust,
debris,
etc.

rescue workers who filed claims asserting respiratory injuries. After the Towers collapsed, hundreds of firefighters and other rescue workers commenced a cleanup operation and search for survivors, enveloped by a cloud of dust and debris allegedly containing asbestos fibers and other toxic substances. During the following days and weeks, those at the site continued to breathe the residue of the disaster. Now they would come knocking at the door of the fund, asking whether their asthma, bronchial congestion, scarred lungs, and other respiratory injuries would be compensable. Fund regulations dealt with these claims. The regulations emphasized that only *physical* injuries were eligible for compensation; mental anguish and post traumatic stress disorder would not be recognized.

*

Kfls
concern

This was a tough call. A strong argument could be made that such mental injury and emotional trauma should be compensable, but I was worried about an open-ended run on the U.S. Treasury. I envisioned 5 million New Yorkers filing claims, as well as the millions of additional Americans and foreigners who watched the disaster unfold on television. Second, I decided that the physical injuries must have occurred in the "immediate vicinity" of the World Trade Center or the Pentagon. The fund would not recognize respiratory claims from New Jersey residents who observed the horror from the other side of the Hudson River and inhaled the dust as it spread beyond the World Trade Center site. Nor would it pay the claim of an elderly woman who was crushed attempting to escape from the scene on the Staten Island Ferry. I had to draw the line of eligibility in a manner that some would undoubtedly view as arbitrary, but I considered essential to the efficiency and credibility of the program.

To draw our map of the affected area, we figured what appeared to be the ambit of likely injury. We asked police and firefighters where people were most at risk. We also used evidence that developed during the three months before the April issuance of our final guidelines— like the information about the airplane engine that landed three blocks from the WTC, which was, therefore, clearly within the ambit of risk. But we needed to define and limit the eligible area of compensation. If we permit- ted Jersey City residents who inhaled the dust and debris to be eligible, we could anticipate millions of additional cases.

In order to reinforce these objectives, the regulations also required that any alleged physical injury had to have been treated by a physician within seventy-two hours after the attacks of September 11. Contemporaneous medical evidence was required to confirm the existence and nature of this treatment. (Exceptions would be made in the case of rescue workers who did not discover their latent respi- ratory injuries until later.) These requirements—physical injury inflicted by the terrorists in the immediate vicinity of the World Trade Center or Pentagon and subsequent contemporary medical treatment—limited the number of serious physical injuries eligible for compensation. We ultimately awarded a little more than $1 billion to 2,682 of the 4,435 individuals who filed claims with the fund.

(See the Appendix at the end of this book for more details.)

Fund regulations also had to deal with issues of due process and fairness. I recognized from my days working on the Agent Orange case that fair procedures and transparency were essential for claimants to become comfortable with the fund. The fund could only be successful if claimants were given the opportunity to be heard. September 11 families and victims had to be convinced that they had a personal stake in the fund and that the program was there to serve them. I was determined to make due process a cardinal virtue of the program.

The detailed process of planning the fund's operations was tricky work. If the regulations were too complex, if the claim form itself was too consumer unfriendly, applicants would be reluctant to apply. Already paralyzed with grief and fear, they'd be easily discouraged from participating in the fund. Nor did we want to intimidate them with too much information. And so we tried to strike a balance, offering them careful guidance on how to apply and informing them what would be considered in the calculation of awards. Within six weeks, we had a set of interim regulations that we considered good enough to make available for public scrutiny and comment.

We also made a concerted effort to create a simple claim form but were not entirely successful. The sheer size of the individual awards required extensive documentation and corroboration to minimize fraud and ensure the accuracy of awards. The claim form ended up running thirty-one pages—long enough to intimidate some traumatized family members and infuriate others.

We also decided to create an immediate emergency fund for 9/11 families and victims in severe financial straits. Convinced that many families would be unable to make their mortgage or car payments or buy groceries, we decided to offer an advance benefit of $50,000 to any eligible family that had lost a loved one on 9/11. We also agreed to advance $25,000 to victims who had been physically injured. We did not require eligible claimants to fill out detailed forms or offer proof of economic loss; these requirements would come later. This was simple, emergency compensation for those in desperate need. Accelerated payments would be deemed a credit against any ultimate award. Surprisingly, only 236 individuals took advantage of this emergency relief. I later learned that private charities had already come to the rescue of most of those who would have qualified for our emergency program.

I also decided that we needed a swift, certain, and uncomplicated formula, clearly explained in the regulations, to estimate individual awards. And so we developed a presumptive economic methodology that any family could use to compute its own award. The key variables were the annual salary and age of the victim and the number of dependents he or she left behind. Although any family could reject this presumptive methodology and ask for detailed individual consideration of its own special economic circumstances, we managed to create a streamlined procedure for families who desired speed and certainty.

This methodology took the form of a set of charts laying out the likely economic compensation that a family could expect. These charts provoked controversy in their own right.

The statute and the regulations we developed make it clear that three fundamental public policy considerations colored the entire program.

First, I was determined to promote *consistency* in awards. Consistency is not the same as uniformity, This point is crucial. I couldn't change the statutory language requiring economic distinctions between stockbrokers and dishwashers. The family of one would receive more than the other. But among all stockbrokers, fund rules were consistently applied. The same with all dishwashers. Perceptions of favoritism or bias would gut the program of any legitimacy and defeat the intentions of Congress in enacting the law. Whether a claimant was represented by a high-powered lawyer or decided to represent herself would have no impact on my ultimate decision. I was a fiduciary for all 9/11 victims and their families. Any definition of fairness and justice required the same rules for all; no individual claimant had an inherent advantage over another. This emphasis on consistency—that the rules would be applied in an equal and fair manner—would help ensure the success of the fund.

Second, I promoted *transparency* in administering the program. Proactive outreach to the families was an important part of this. The emphasis on transparency

transparency

KFls *discretion*

governed all key decisions made by the fund. Once we decided on a course of action we notified the families in person at community town hall meetings, and we posted our decisions on our website to ensure the widest possible dissemination. Critically important decisions about eligibility and compensation would not be made by some faceless bureaucrat sitting behind closed doors in an antiseptic Washington government office. There would be no secret deals or hidden agendas. I thought of President Woodrow Wilson and the formula he advocated during the Paris Peace Talks at the close of World War I—open covenants, openly arrived at.

Finally, I was convinced that I should use my discretion to *narrow the gap* between high-end and low-end awards. Although the statute prohibited me from awarding the same amount to all claimants, Congress had protected itself by conferring undefined discretion on a special master. This discretion became my talisman. I believed it important that the national public support for 9/11 victims and their families found in the statute not be undercut by class distinctions reflected in widely divergent awards. Senator Kennedy provided me some very thoughtful advice: "Ken, just make sure that 15 percent of the families don't receive 85 percent of the taxpayers' money." Pure economic loss calculations might call for the family of a Cantor Fitzgerald bond trader or Keefe Bruyette banker to receive double digit millions from the fund, even after deductions, but I would reduce such awards. Similarly, I would use my discretion to make sure that the survivors of an undocumented dishwasher or the family of a soldier killed at the Pentagon received more than rote application of the statutory formula called for.

This clearly constituted a type of "social engineering." Understandably, it would prove difficult and controversial.

The next crucial phase of our job was to launch an outreach program. I knew that some private 9/11 charities had declined to meet with family representatives. Instead, officials of these charities simply announced that they had drawn up rules and regulations for disbursing charitable donations, thereby making face-to-face meetings with the families unnecessary and counterproductive. I understood the motivations of the charity directors. Why get embroiled in emotional personal confrontations that might end up fueling accusations of favoritism toward families that received larger payments? But I also thought this arm's-length policy was a mistake. It meant that the families didn't understand how the $2.7 billion in charitable giving would be distributed, and a certain mistrust developed between the groups.

I was determined to avoid opening a gap between donors and receivers. For the 9/11 fund to achieve its goal of speedily compensating eligible families and victims, marketing and publicizing the fund would be essential. Families needed to know about the program, its requirements and benefits, what it could do and not do under the statute. I immediately implemented two outreach plans.

First, with the help of my technical experts, we established a user-friendly website, updated regularly, which posted frequently asked questions about the program and provided readily understandable answers. This website became a valuable vehicle for educating the public about the program and about the decisions I was making.

Second, I decided to reach out to the families, to become the visible symbol of the Victim Compensation Fund by meeting with them, even in their moments of deepest grief.

Within a few weeks my core team had crafted interim regulations governing the program as well as a draft application form for families and victims to read—close to a hundred pages of information. Many had questions about these regulations, and they became one focus of the meetings. We had staffers at our town hall meetings giving out copies of these documents; families could also download them from the Internet or request copies by mail. At the meetings, some people were seeing the regulations for the first time, some had seen them on the Web, and some were experts, prepared with specific questions about specific subparagraphs.

For a year I lived out of a suitcase, conducting meetings at schools, community centers, hotels, and town halls in Manhattan, Staten Island, Long Island, Jersey City, and other locations in New Jersey, various locations in Connecticut, Boston, Philadelphia, and Crystal City in Virginia. I even made two trips to California to meet with victims' families as well as two trips to London to meet with the families of British citizens. Members of the Senate and House—Senators Hillary Clinton, Jon Corzine, and Ted Kennedy, and House members Marge Roukema, Steve Israel, Peter King, Carolyn McCarthy, Chris Shays, and Rush Holt, helped organize and run the meetings. We held over a hundred meetings in nine months.

For the convenience of the families, we held meetings during the day, on evenings, and on weekends. Each session lasted from one and a half to three hours. I would extend the meetings as long as people still had questions, but sometimes I had to break away, saying, "I have to be at another meeting—please write or e-mail me or talk to my staff members who will remain behind, or see me when I come back in two weeks."

I came to the meetings prepared with important substantive information about the statute, the regulations, and the exercise of my discretion. For example, many families had heard about the life insurance and other offsets that were required, under the terms of the law, to be deducted from their fund payments. Some who'd been provided with generous benefits by their employers or who'd had the foresight to buy large life insurance policies were worried that these offsets would reduce their awards to zero—in effect penalizing them for prudent financial planning. I told them not to worry; I planned to exercise my discretion to guarantee that any claimant, regardless of offsets required by the statute, would receive no less than $250,000 simply by applying to the fund.

This decision made sense in the context of the fund's

broader purpose. Remember, the statute was intended to create a fair alternative to lawsuits. Why would a family that expected to receive nothing under the fund because of the collateral offset requirement even bother to apply? Such families would have nothing to lose in filing a lawsuit if the fund formulas provided them no incentive to enter the program. The guaranteed $250,000 payment became minimum compensation for participating in the fund. And, I emphasized, it was only a *minimum*; present me with additional exceptional circumstances and I would increase the award. (As it turned out, I almost always did so, increasing the minimum payment to as much as $1 million in a few cases.)

In these group meetings, I also had a less pleasing message to deliver. I had to dash expectations that the families of wealthy wage earners would received tens of millions of dollars. I pulled no punches. I made it very clear— much to the anger of some high-income survivors and their representatives, like Howard Lutnik, chairman of the board and chief executive officer of Cantor Fitzgerald— that payouts in the double-digit millions (or anything close to that) were extremely unlikely. Instead, I would exercise my discretion to reduce the gap between high-income and low-income families. If a calculation based on lost income resulted in a figure of $10, $20, or $50 million after offsets, I would reduce the award to an amount I believed was more reasonable and in line with what Congress intended. Although there were no absolute award ceilings (this would violate the statute), I spelled out again and again that awards exceeding $3 million would be "exceedingly rare," and would require "extraordinary circumstances."

Nonetheless some families of high-wage earners equated 9/11 awards with their existing lifestyle. I heard many comments like, "Who are you, Mr. Feinberg, to tell me that a $20 million award is excessive, unfair, and unreasonable? Have you visited my home on Long Island or my apartment in New York City to see for yourself how I live? How dare you!"

My determination to address this issue head-on provoked intense criticism. Some family members took the microphone during town hall meetings to denounce me as "arrogant" and "insensitive" because I was unwilling to validate the economic arguments advanced by the wealthy families.

I also began to take heat over grievances that were fundamentally unrelated to my work on behalf of the 9/11 fund. Because I was highly visible, families began to view me as a representative of the U.S. government. Consequently I became an outlet for all their anger arising out of 9/11, including their anger over the government's failure to prevent the attacks. Unable to meet with the president of the United States or the CIA or FBI director, families turned to me with their questions: "What did the president know about the pending terrorist attacks, and when did he know it?" "Mr. Feinberg, my son is dead because the CIA was asleep at the switch. Why?" "My daughter died at the Pentagon because the FBI failed to do a better job of monitoring the conduct of the terrorists once they entered the United States. Why?"

These questions often led to an attack on my personal integrity and the 9/11 fund. "Aren't you here today, Mr. Feinberg, merely to provide us hush money so we won't ask tough questions and pursue our own individual investigations into the causes of the 9/11 tragedy?"

It hurt to be subjected to these kinds of attacks. Deep inside, I knew they were unfair. But I refused to engage in a public debate over the criticism. I constantly reminded myself that the fund was not about me. Instead, I tried to take a philosophical attitude. Harsh criticism came with the job, and no matter what decisions I made, I could never satisfy everyone.

In retrospect, I can see that I might have handled some of those early confrontations better. In some ways, my legal training and experience had prepared me ideally for this challenge. I knew how to weigh the complexities of such a compensation program and administer it fairly. But in other ways, nothing could have prepared me for working with the 9/11 families. In my past cases, even those freighted with powerful emotions, such as Agent Orange, I'd dealt mainly with my fellow lawyers, usually in a courtroom setting years after the traumatic events that resulted in the lawsuit. Now I was talking directly with victimized families within days or weeks of the unprecedented national tragedy.

Not surprisingly, the communication style I'd developed over the years proved less than ideal for this new challenge. I tend to be straightforward and businesslike, especially when I'm trying to explain a complex plan to a group of lawyers. My preferred approach is to dive in head first: "Hello, ladies and gentlemen. I'm here to explain how the 9/11 fund will work. Please hold your questions; we'll allow plenty of time for those later. Let's start at the beginning. The statute authorizes the following procedures..."

I should have realized that this kind of neutral, authoritative, purely factual presentation would strike the 9/11 families as brusque and callous. Instead, it took me a while to realize the effect I was having and adjust my approach. Looking back, I should have started every meeting in a quieter, more empathetic way—expressing sympathy, offering words of respect and condolence, and inviting the families to start the conversation: "I'm here on behalf of the people of the United States to offer our help to you in this terribly painful time. What do you need? What can we do to make it easier for you to cope?" I suspect that, after a period of emotional venting and sharing of sympathies, the 9/11 families would have been more ready to settle into a dispassionate discussion of the nuts and bolts of the program.

I committed a couple of genuine faux pas during the early town hall meetings. On one occasion, when trying to stress the uniqueness of the 9/11 fund, I remarked, "This program is not business as usual." Eyes got wide in the audience, and some family members exchanged glances. Then a stricken husband got to his feet and angrily retorted, "This is not a *business* you're talking about, Mr. Feinberg. You're talking about my *wife*."

Another time, I was urging a group of Staten Islanders to participate in the fund rather than mount lawsuits, a path I was convinced would lead nowhere. To emphasize my conviction, I told the families, "This is the only real game in town." As soon as the words escaped my lips, I caught a glimpse of my lieutenant, Camille Biros, wincing in the front row of the audience. With a sinking feeling, I realized what I'd said. The room practically erupted in anger. One outraged wife spoke for the group. "To you, this may be a game," she spat. "But not to us." Heads nodded around the room.

What could I do? I apologized profusely and inwardly vowed to never, ever use that kind of language again. I never did.

After that meeting, one particularly angry member of the audience confronted me in the hallway. "I see that your name is Feinberg. Well, we don't need *your kind* on Staten Island," he said.

Encounters like that were rare. I quickly learned from my early missteps, the result of on-the-job training. I became more conciliatory and understanding, and toned down my businesslike demeanor with a softer, more sympathetic and understanding approach. How could I, or anyone, not be touched by the grief and anger the 9/11 families were experiencing?

What made the job even more challenging were the new and unpredictable emotional and intellectual challenges I confronted every day. In one typical twenty-four-hour day, I met with a group of foreign worker families in lower Manhattan and then traveled to Times Square to attend a rowdy gathering of over six hundred Cantor Fitzgerald families at the Marriot Marquis Hotel. The next morning I drove through a snowstorm to Basking Ridge, New Jersey, where I met with a group of twenty suburban widows; then on to Stamford, Connecticut, for a gathering with those who'd lost high-wage earner spouses.

Not all the town hall meetings were bitter or confrontational. Actually their atmosphere and tone varied dramatically depending on the location. In New York, anger and frustration usually boiled over. Families demanded greater compensation. Sometimes, they attacked me personally. "I spit on you and your children," said the widow of one firefighter, incensed that she was receiving less money because of life insurance offsets.

Many New Yorkers seemed to feel that their justifiable anger over the attacks entitled them to increased payment, as if the money was a form of reparations for the failure of the federal government to protect its citizens. This attitude became apparent when I hosted a series of group meetings in the basement of my law firm's Manhattan office building on East 49th Street. We gathered in a large, movie-style auditorium reserved for tenant conferences. One day I would meet with as many as two hundred families of New York City firefighters and policemen, the next day with Cantor Fitzgerald spouses, a third day with the families of foreign workers or members of a Hispanic or Korean 9/11 family association.

Informality and casual attire characterized these meetings. I welcomed the guests and explained the program and the limitations imposed on me by the statute. I tried to anticipate the most obvious questions about eligibility and compensation. To encourage a candid exchange of views, I made it clear that these sessions with the families were off the record (no transcript or tape recordings were made of the discussion).

All seemed well until I invited questions from the audience. Then the floodgate opened, releasing a torrent of invective and anger aimed directly at me. It became very personal. "Mr. Feinberg, you have discretion. So exercise it and give us our due," one family member said. Family after family accused me of devaluing the life of a husband or daughter, of failing to recognize the victim's true worth, of engaging in a coldhearted calculation of dollars and cents when I should be focusing on the uniqueness and human qualities of the deceased. "How can you be so insensitive, so detached, so unwilling to understand the human qualities of my dead wife? How can the government be so callous?" one survivor shouted.

It was tough to stay calm when barraged by these attacks. But I realized that a raised voice or an angry rejoinder would only heighten tensions and provoke an even stronger reaction in the room. I also knew that if I buckled under the pressure and promised what I couldn't deliver, I'd create worse problems in the long run. So I pledged to listen to every argument, to respond with understanding and sympathy to every complaint, and to extend the meetings as long as necessary for everyone to be heard.

My willingness to stand up to the criticism from family members reinforcing each other's confrontational attitudes eventually led to a more substantive discussion of the program. It was as if the families, after venting their frustration and anger at me, then acknowledged the necessity of quietly and calmly learning more about the program. The meetings ended with a promise to reconvene the group for further discussion. More than one family member would take me aside before leaving the building to quietly thank me for listening and expressing support. "And I'm sorry, Mr. Feinberg," they'd often add, "for what you had to put up with during the meeting. I know you're only trying to help."

In Virginia, the environment could not have been more different. Dealing with military families almost guaranteed a certain degree of respect and military decorum. I learned that military families develop a certain insularity, especially in times of grief, and circle the wagons to provide each other emotional comfort and support. They seemed to speak with one voice, recognizing that, as military families, they stood with their lost loved ones in harm's way. They rarely asked a personal question pertaining to their own individual circumstances; instead, they focused on issues of general importance to the entire group.

The tone of the Virginia meetings was remarkably civil. "Sir, I have a question," was the common introductory phrase when I met with the families in a hotel room less than a mile from the Pentagon. "Thank you" was almost always the response after my answer. There were no invectives, no indictments, no demands; instead, a collective hush fell over the gathering. A series of reasonable questions followed concerning the technicalities of the program. How would I treat military housing and travel allowances in calculating awards? Would I take into account the likelihood of the victim receiving a military promotion? How would I treat military pensions and anticipated battle pay? Occasionally I heard the sound of stifled weeping in the crowd.

At the conclusion of one meeting attended by about two hundred people, I was presented a framed certificate of thanks from the Pentagon families. I was touched and expressed my deep appreciation, explaining to the families that their act of kindness was a first in my administration of the fund. I reminded them that we were all in this together. Although I could never stand in their shoes or fully appreciate the measure of their loss, I would do all I could to vindicate their trust in me. They were grateful for the government's largesse and they thanked me warmly for my willingness to visit them and explain the program.

California was different still. There wasn't the hot New York anger or the calm Pentagon respect. Instead, when I visited Sacramento for a town hall meeting of a hundred family representatives in a local hotel, a series of questions were followed by a request to join hands and say a prayer together.

My experience with the families in California can best be described as a type of public demonstration of grief and reconciliation. It was as if the families had chosen to deal with the 9/11 tragedy by suppressing individual protestations of life's unfairness and joining together. "We" replaced "I." "We have questions for you, Mr. Feinberg," they said. "And we grieve together." I was impressed by this display of public emotion designed to reinforce individual resolve. But I felt a bit awkward. I wasn't really prepared for this type of collective response. Although I tried to become part of the group mentality, I had difficulty identifying with this cohesive approach to grief. Oddly enough, I was more comfortable in the combative world of New York City or the polite, respectful Pentagon environment.

But when the community meetings ended and I met privately with individual families in Sacramento, Los Angeles, and San Francisco, it quickly became apparent that there was nothing unique about their grief, loss, and worry about the future. These individual meetings raised the same issues about the fund, whether in New York, Virginia, or California. Personal issues quickly came to the fore, overshadowing any community-wide response to my visits. When I met with individual families, it all became very *personal*—what did the fund mean to a particular family grieving over the loss of a loved one.

My London meetings with British families revealed a fresh problem—an understandable sense of general skepticism about the fund on the part of foreign claimants. The uniqueness of the program, the unmatched generosity of the American people, often left foreign claimants literally speechless. "Only in America," they would whisper. When I explained the program to thirty British families gathered in a large conference room in central London and mentioned awards averaging $2 million, I could sense the disbelief in the room. I was quickly peppered with questions: "Do we have to surrender our English citizenship to become eligible for compensation?" "Do we have to travel to the United States to collect our money?" "Do we have to surrender our passports before receiving a check?" Despite my reassuring responses, the families remained incredulous. "You mean to tell us, Mr. Feinberg, that your government is prepared to give each of us an average of $2 million because of the death of our sons and daughters. What's the catch?" It took months before foreign claimants from England and sixty-six other foreign nations became sufficiently comfortable with the program to file claims.

On rare occasions, I was accompanied at the town hall meetings by local officials or members of Congress. Usually they stayed away, leaving me alone to weather the storm of protests. When they did accompany me, they were not spared family outbursts.

Once Marge Roukema, a member of Congress from New Jersey, organized a meeting at a local town hall in her congressional district. Over 150 people attended. In the midst of the question-and-answer period, one woman rose to complain, "Mr. Feinberg, I am outraged that you are offsetting my husband's life insurance before you render an award. We were responsible about planning for our financial future. Now you're penalizing us. It's very unfair."

Before I could respond, Representative Roukema jumped in. Turning to me, she declared, "Let me just say that I could not agree more. I find it an outrage that you would penalize people with life insurance."

The woman in the audience turned red. "Congresswoman, how dare you criticize Mr. Feinberg like that! These life insurance offsets aren't *his* fault. They're spelled out in the law—the law *you* voted for!"

Roukema was nonplussed. Searching for a response, she mumbled something about how the law had been rushed through Congress: "We didn't have a chance to read every line." And she promised to introduce an amendment in Congress to change the law.

I tried to come to her defense, explaining how prompt congressional action was essential in enacting the new law. But I did not want the families to nurture any false hopes. "I wish the congresswoman well in her effort to change the law. But the fact is that there isn't a prayer of the law being changed. I have no choice but to deal with it the way it was written, and do the best I can under the circumstances." Heads nodded around the room.

I know that Senator Corzine proposed an amendment in the Senate that would have eliminated the life insurance offsets. As I correctly predicted, it died in committee.

These months of town hall meetings were grueling for me and for my staff. But I'm glad they took place. I believe that giving the 9/11 families direct access to me and my staff helped put a human face on the program. At least we showed that the fund was not being administered by some technician or bureaucrat in Washington but by Kenneth Feinberg—an individual who wanted to understand these families in distress and was determined to use his power to help.

CHAPTER THREE

From Theory to Reality

THE AWESOME authority vested in me was not subject
to judicial review or congressional oversight. My
appointment by the attorney general was not even subject
to Senate confirmation. The only check on my unprecedented authority was the day-to-day oversight of my
boss, the attorney general. But John Ashcroft and I both
knew that this oversight was more theoretical than real—
that an attorney general stretched to the limit in our
post–9/11 world would have little time to monitor my
daily activities in compensating victims.

From the start, I viewed this power as both a blessing
and a curse. True, I could administer the program free
from bureaucratic interference and red tape; I could
establish a compensation scheme that reflected exactly
what I believed. But the broad language of the statute
also guaranteed that I would become the outlet for every
family criticism, every gripe. This expectation quickly

turned into reality when I launched the town hall meeting program.

But even as I was reaching out to the 9/11 families and the general public to explain and defend the program, my staff and I were also wrestling with the daunting legal, economic, and political questions that neither the original statute nor our interim regulations had fully settled.

One of the hardest parts of my job was dealing with questions about eligibility for the program from grieving families with relatives who died in the 1995 Oklahoma City bombing of the Murrah Federal Building. They asked questions like, "Why not me? Didn't my wife die from a terrorist attack? Where's my money?" And what about the families who lost loved ones in the 1998 terrorist bombing of the U.S. embassy in Kenya? What about the anthrax victims in the Washington, D.C., area? And the navy victims of the terrorist attack on the USS *Cole*? What could I say to the pregnant wife of *Wall Street Journal* reporter Daniel Pearl, when she requested a hearing seeking compensation for the death of her husband, killed by terrorists in Pakistan?

And what about the victims of the first terrorist attack on the World Trade Center in 1993? New York's Chuck Schumer approached me in the halls of the Senate and urged me to find some way to compensate the eight families who lost loved ones in that incident. "Ken, it's not fair," he said. "Surely you can include the 1993 families in your program. The attack was committed by the very same people. Can't you find a way to compensate these families?"

Although I empathized with Schumer and the families whose interests he represented, the statute that governed my work was clear. The fund applied only to lives lost and injured in the 9/11 attacks. I couldn't compensate families of victims of previous terrorist attacks, just as I couldn't compensate families who had lost loved ones in other circumstances—in a flood, fire, or other natural disaster.

Every year, some Americans die as heros, rescuing fellow citizens from burning buildings or swollen rivers. Some lose their lives while coming to the aid of robbery victims. Others are random victims of death, killed in hit-and-run accidents or critically injured in automobile collisions caused by drunk drivers. A few families whose members were victimized in these ways contacted us, asking for compensation. But all were ineligible. I was constrained by a statute expressly limited to 9/11 victims. Their gripe was with Congress, not with me.

This doesn't mean that the law as passed was fair to all victims of life's misfortunes. Obviously, it wasn't. The statute picked a chosen few for unprecedented public generosity. Why should some citizens receive millions in public compensation while others—also innocent victims—received nothing? The latter viewed the statute as very arbitrary.

I wished I had a more satisfying answer to offer the unhappy families who questioned me about this. I sought an explanation in the congressional debates and legislative history underlying the new law. I searched in vain for a rationale that justified providing favored treatment to some but not others. Was such a program consistent with American notions of democracy, egalitarianism, and equal protection of the law? Elitism is not a conspicuous American trait. Our public programs involving education, health care, and other basic benefits frown on arbitrary distinctions. Yet, in its eligibility criteria and generosity, the 9/11 fund carried the notion of elitism to new heights.

Then there were the questions about who should receive payment on behalf of an eligible victim. In drafting our interim regulations, we considered the rights of an engaged person or same-sex partner of the victim. As with other types of intrafamily disputes, we decided to apply state law to determine who could speak for the deceased. But no states, except, perhaps, Vermont, Hawaii, and California, recognized the legal rights of engaged persons, non-family members or significant others. In the absence of a will, just about every state would prevent the same-sex partner or engaged person from recovery and would, instead, recognize the victim's biological parents as eligible beneficiaries.

But in speaking with some of the 9/11 families, we began to uncover complications. In some cases, for example, the parents had been estranged from the victim. Under my regulations, those parents would receive a windfall at the expense of the same-sex partner or fiancée. On the surface, this seemed unfair. But I had no firsthand knowledge of who had the better of the argument. I wasn't a family counselor who could probe for the truth or order an investigation to discover the facts. I didn't have the time or the mandate to referee such disputes and declare the appropriate beneficiary.

As the program began to take concrete shape, I realized that cases like these were appropriate opportunities for me to exercise the discretion given me by the law. I would intervene and mediate by urging the parents and the same-sex partner or fiancée to come to an agreement on issues of eligibility and distribution. I began delaying the distribution of funds until family members had worked out their differences. In most cases, I convinced the parties to agree on an allocation of the award.

Sometimes, however, family peace required that I add an additional amount and earmark it solely for the fiancée or same-sex partner. Only then would the victim's parents agree to a consensual division of the award. On a few occasions, even this did not work; the parents promised to litigate if the fiancée or same-sex partner received any part of the award. There was just too much bad blood. Ultimately, in about two dozen cases, conflicting claims would have to be determined in state courts.

I also found that determining the meaning of local law could prove problematic, particularly in cases involving the foreign citizens from fifty-nine nations who died on 9/11. What did the law of India require, or the law of Malaysia? Determining and applying the relevant laws wasn't easy, particularly when foreign laws were inconsistent with American law. For example, there was simply no way I would agree to comply with foreign laws that prohibited women from receiving any portion of the victim's estate. Nor would I as a matter of public policy recognize foreign laws that endorsed the legality of multiple wives. In such cases, I would exercise my discretion to modify the law of a foreign nation when it came to the distribution of 9/11 awards.

There was also the troublesome issue surrounding the money raised for 9/11 families by private charities. Never before had any disaster triggered such generous private giving by the American people. When the New York Times Foundation launched a solicitation drive in the newspaper, it anticipated private donor contributions of $2–3 million. Instead, the foundation received over $60 million during the first three months after 9/11. In total, charities raised over $2.7 billion for the 9/11 families.

Jack Rosenthal, the head of the New York Times Foundation, coined the phrase "vengeful philanthropy" to help explain this unprecedented generosity. The American people were determined to demonstrate the nation's cohesiveness and resolve to the terrorists, their allies, and the world. The terrorists might destroy material symbols of American might and kill or injure thousands, but they could not undermine the will and solidarity of America as a nation. In this way giving to the 9/11 charities was an act of national defiance.

It was wonderful that Americans had given so much to help their fellow citizens. But it created a dilemma for me. Should the amounts received by the families be deducted from their fund awards? A strong argument could be made that, according to the statute, *all* other sources of income, including charitable donations, ought to be offset. But when I met in New York City with representatives of the United Way, the American Red Cross, the Twin Towers Fund, and some twenty-five other charities, they ganged up on me. "Why should we subsidize your government fund?" they asked. "That's not what our donors intended. If you insist on subtracting charitable gifts," they told me, "we'll simply delay the distribution of our funds until after you issue your awards. We can hold off as long as you like."

Recognizing that any delay in the distribution of charitable proceeds to 9/11 families was politically untenable, I blinked. I had no choice. I decreed that money received by 9/11 families from private charities would not be considered as collateral income and would not be deducted from fund awards.

Was I bending the letter of the law? Sure. But making a practical decision for the benefit of the families was more important than rigidly adhering to the ambiguous wording of a quickly drafted, hastily passed statute. This was the right choice.

As I met with the 9/11 families at town hall meetings, they were faced with the raw truth that each claimant would receive a different award depending on the economic wherewithal of the victim. Many reacted with resentment, anger, and disbelief. Widows of firefighters and military men could not understand why they would receive less from the fund than the stockbrokers' widows.

Why was the government devaluing the lives of the heros at the World Trade Center and the Pentagon by awarding more to wealthier civilians?

I explained that the methodology was based on the statute itself, which required different awards for each claimant and demanded consideration of economic loss. But this did not sit well with police, firefighter, and military families. "You have discretion," was the retort. "You can make it right." I promised to consider individual circumstances, but I emphasized that I couldn't change the law with the wave of some magic wand.

In any case, the ethical and philosophical issues aren't as clear-cut as they might appear to a grieving family seeking validation for the life of their loved one. If good Samaritanism is to be rewarded, shouldn't the firefighter at the World Trade Center or soldier at the Pentagon receive more than the stockbroker or airplane pilot? But Congress had decided to base compensation on the economic wherewithal of the victim. Was this fair? On ABC's *Nightline,* former governor Frank Keating of Oklahoma said no. "We in this state would not have contemplated distribution based upon income and lifetime earnings, because that would simply be un-American."

Sounds inarguable at first blush. But is it? The most sacrosanct of all entitlement programs, social security, is based on what you earn. Different contributions, and consequently different payments, are mandated by law depending on individual earning capacity. Is it really "un-American" to award $500,000 to the family of a 9/11 victim with annual earnings of $20,000 as a busboy, while providing $2 million to the survivors of a stockbroker at the World Trade Center earning $3 million per year?

Juries make similar decisions every day in every city, town, and village of our nation. America's free market system and its reliance on individual choice to fulfill personal potential would seem to require that public compensation make such distinctions. The 9/11 statute simply reflects and reinforces the economic status of the victim at the time of death. Based on this argument, differential fund awards are as American as apple pie.

But even the wealthier families quarreled with our draft regulations. The charts we created to help families estimate their awards showed varying levels of annual earnings that topped out at $231,000. Above this amount, the charts showed only a series of asterisks. An arbitrary cutoff? Not really. According to calculations by the Bureau of Labor Statistics, 98 percent of all wage earners in America earn less than $231,000 annually. Furthermore, earnings above that amount tend to be speculative, uncertain, and highly variable from year to year, including not just wages but stock options, bonuses, and other extraordinary payments. Consequently it was hard to justify applying a standard lifetime earnings formula to the high-income victims who'd been earning more than $231,000 a year.

I labored to explain this logic clearly and concisely. But the high-income families would have none of it. At a meeting involving Cantor Fitzgerald families, speaker after speaker criticized me for discriminating against high-income families by not recognizing their incredible wage-earning capabilities. I promised I would carefully review the claims of wealthy families. That failed to placate my critics. "Use the discretion the statute gives you," demanded one widow. "It's very unfair to limit your automatic awards to $231,000."

The truth is that any economic loss isn't easily quantifiable. It has to include estimated *future* earnings, a crystal ball exercise that's as much art as science. Juries attempt such calculations every day, but they do so collectively and out of the public eye. The spotlight was now on me and me alone—a visible and inviting target. The decisions I had to make were excruciating. Would a young associate in a law firm have eventually become a partner, thereby quadrupling his income? Would a young stockbroker have enjoyed as good a year in 2002 as she had in 2000? Would the corporal at the Pentagon have been promoted to captain? And after leaving the service, would he have found success in the private sector? What about the up-and-coming bond trader who garnered record bonuses in the Clinton years—would she have been as successful when the economy turned sour? And what about the college student just beginning his career—what kind of success would he achieve? Who could say? I would make a good faith effort to distinguish speculation from reality, but I could not account for all of life's uncertainties.

In the emotional climate surrounding the 9/11 fund, every decision I made was almost guaranteed to anger someone. I proposed an experiment to disappointed family members: "Offer the same economic facts to ten different people and ask them all to calculate a fair award. I guarantee you they'll come up with ten different amounts." No one took me up on my challenge. I was offering logic, but logic didn't ease their hurt.

Then there was the question of noneconomic loss—the pain and suffering of the 9/11 victims on the airplanes, at the World Trade Center and Pentagon, and the emotional distress inflicted on their families. A public meeting I hosted in my New York office highlighted the emotional fragility associated with such calculations.

I invited a broadly representative group of over one hundred surviving spouses to come to the meeting to share their opinions about how we should calculate noneconomic loss. The meeting quickly turned into an emotional tug-of-war among the families.

One widow explained that her husband had telephoned her numerous times while trapped at the World Trade Center: "My husband called to say good-bye, to tell me that he loved me, to tell me to take care of the kids." This widow argued that she deserved more money as a result. "I am entitled to more noneconomic loss than a wife whose husband was killed instantly. My husband suffered more, and so did I."

Another widow argued that she lost her husband after thirty-six years of marriage and therefore was the victim of more emotional distress than the widow who had only been married for six months. This did not sit well with newlyweds. As one widow put it, "I was only married for six months, but I loved my husband every bit as much as you did. How dare you argue that you suffered more!"

Others maintained that lost loved ones on the airplanes suffered more. They had witnessed the terrorists seize the planes and direct them toward their targets, thereby experiencing the horror of knowing their deaths were imminent. Surely, argued their surviving families, more noneconomic loss was justified for such pain and suffering.

The cacophony of arguments validated my original preference: to refuse to evaluate individual suffering. Instead, the interim regulations had stipulated that noneconomic loss awards would be the same for all claimants: $250,000 for the pain and suffering of all 9/11 dead, and $50,000 for the emotional distress inflicted on each surviving spouse and dependent. I'd picked the $250,000 number because of precedents in long-established federal law governing death benefit payments to police officers and firefighters, as well as subsidized life insurance payments made to survivors of the military personnel killed in action. Despite the conflicting claims from various family groups, I decided to stick to the one-size-fits-all approach to noneconomic loss in the final regulations.

Suddenly the warring claimants were united—in denouncing the stinginess of my payments. "In airplane crash cases, pain and suffering awards are in the millions" argued one individual at a family meeting on Staten Island. "Why won't you pay us what a jury would have awarded if we had sued?"

"Because this is not a lawsuit," I replied. "It's an alternative to a lawsuit created by Congress. Besides," I explained, "for every jury award you might cite, I could cite another where a jury found no liability and awarded no damages at all."

I'm sure that my arguments didn't completely satisfy the 9/11 families. But I did decide to increase the $50,000 payment for each surviving spouse and dependent to $100,000. This brought the final payments for noneconomic loss more in line with the expectations of the families and muted the criticisms leveled at the fund.

I made many other decisions that proved controversial. For example, the presumptive formula did not recognize the emotional distress suffered by the parents of a 9/11 victim unless they were found to be dependents. The fund needed some limitations, and refusing to compensate nondependent parents was a reasonable place to draw the line. But this decision proved to be a source of consternation when families came to visit me. "Tell me, Mr. Feinberg," I was asked again and again, "why does your formula not recognize the grief and sorrow we are experiencing over the loss of our child?" I explained the rationale for my decision as best I could, but I doubt I convinced many suffering parents.

Many people also complained about the charts we created to help surviving families estimate their approximate awards. As I've noted, some high-end families felt that these charts were unfair because they didn't establish presumptive awards above an annual income of $231,000. Other families, whether wealthy or of moderate means, found the charts themselves distasteful—a callous attempt to calculate the value of a human life through a cut-and-dried, mechanical formula. This reaction was probably inevitable. It's true that no table of numbers can capture the uniqueness of an individual—which is why we were scrupulous about inviting and considering families' personal input before making any final award. The charts, we always emphasized, were merely a first step in the process, never the final arbiter.

On balance, the charts proved to be a useful tool. They promoted transparency, beaming sunlight onto an otherwise murky and complex set of mathematical calculations and economic methodologies. By helping families understand the relative range of awards and what they could expect if they filed with the fund, the charts encouraged families to communicate with the fund and, ultimately, decide to participate.

During our first three months of meetings, we realized that many families felt unable to decide whether or not to participate in the fund because of lingering uncertainties about the likely size of a payout. A rough approximation drawn from a chart wasn't enough to convince them that forgoing a lawsuit would be in their long-term interest. To alleviate this concern, I announced that any eligible family members could ask to see me to get some idea of the size of their award either before a claim was filed with the fund or at least before the claim was deemed "substantially complete," which constituted a commitment to participate and a rejection of the lawsuit route. Based on individual circumstances, I would give them a "guesstimate," a range within which the award would likely fall.

This process became an important safety valve, softening the perception that anonymous fund functionaries merely crunched numbers without taking into account individual family circumstances. The right to a hearing made the Fund more personal, more friendly, and more attuned to the needs of the 9/11 families. Knowing that they could meet with a real person responsible for the calculation of awards released steam from the emotional pressure cooker. Families knew they could be heard.

These individual family meetings proved to be calmer and more constructive than the more boisterous group meetings, where angry participants fanned the flames of one another's anger and frustration. Many family members who were reluctant to pose questions during public meetings felt more comfortable in private. Tales of extraordinary family dilemmas came tumbling out. At one hastily arranged emergency meeting held in my New York office, a widow told me about her terminal cancer; she wanted to request an expedited 9/11 fund payment so she could care for her children before she died. At another meeting, a young woman tearfully told me how her fiancé's parents, so thoughtful and kind before 9/11, now hung up the phone when she called. At yet another meeting, two grandparents asked my help in securing visitation rights to see grandchildren from whom they'd been separated by a bitter daughter-in-law since 9/11.

Behind all these sorrowful requests and angry demands was one constant refrain: *Why did it happen? And why us?*

By early spring of 2002, applications started pouring into the office. PriceWaterhouseCoopers set up shop in Virginia, just across the Potomac from Washington, D.C. The PWC staff, which eventually numbered over four hundred, became a critical arm of the program, administering claims, reviewing the numbers, and calculating initial award amounts. The calculations were complicated. Assessing a single application often took weeks or months and might include reviewing tax returns, W–2 wage and tax statements, pension plans, 401(k) individual retirement accounts, life insurance contracts, social security disability and death benefit payments, workers' compensation awards, commission and bonus statements, stock options, and onetime employer death payments made to the victim's family and masked as "charitable contributions." Missing documentation further delayed the process.

And those were just the civilians. Computing awards for military personnel was even more complicated. I quickly discovered that the military has its own form of in-kind compensation, financial benefits involving housing, travel allowance payments, battle pay, and life insurance. These and other benefits unique to the military would require special treatment.

Then there were the families of the victims who were foreign nationals who were working in the United States. Some of these individuals found it difficult and sometimes impossible to obtain the necessary financial documentation and information from banks and businesses overseas.

Simply locating the families of foreign nationals living in Ecuador, the Dominican Republic, Colombia, Ghana, and other foreign nations proved startlingly difficult. I started by asking foreign embassies for assistance. They proved unhelpful, not because they opposed the fund but because they were understandably skeptical about the program and its generosity: "Do you mean to say, Mr. Feinberg, that the American people want to provide the family of one of our nationals who died on 9/11 around $2 million? Are you serious?"

The U.S. State Department was more helpful, cabling embassies and consulate offices for their assistance in locating the foreign families:

As many foreign national injured victims or the family members of deceased victims have not yet applied, the Department has been asked to assist the U.S. Department of Justice to ensure that: 1) foreign victims or families of deceased victims of the September 11 tragedy are aware of the fund; 2) they are aware of the impending deadline (December 22, 2003) for application to the Fund; and 3) that they have information about how to contact the program representatives to file an application. . . . DOJ has asked [Consular Affairs] to assist in reaching out to the victims or family members of victims that they have identified as residing overseas to ensure that these individuals are informed of the availability of compensation, the impending deadline for application, and how to apply to the program. DOJ's Office of the Special Master has provided [Consular Affairs] with a list of known victims and contact information for this purpose.

Soon, the Department will forward to the consular sections of selected Embassies a list (provided by the Department of Justice) of victims or family members of victims who have not applied for compensation and who are thought to reside within that country. Posts will be asked: 1) to reach out to these victims via a letter by July 15, 2003 (the letter will be provided with the list); and 2) to inform the Department of the specific results of these efforts, including which individual posts could not reach.

State Department personnel residing in these foreign nations used their good offices to track down eligible families and urge them to file with the fund. Their efforts proved very successful. It appears today that families of every known foreign national who died or was physically injured on 9/11 were located and paid.

There was also the problem of how the fund should

treat the eleven undocumented workers who died in the World Trade Center. The statute declared them eligible. But locating the families of undocumented workers and convincing them to file without fear of deportation or imprisonment proved difficult. I was determined, however, to make every effort to locate such families and convince them to participate, since they needed the compensation more than most.

I implemented a comprehensive outreach effort to reach these families. We translated applications and formal regulations into Spanish, Korean, and other languages in an effort to explain the program. I personally visited local communities in New York City accompanied by a translator. I also relied on local community organizations who could help locate eligible families and urge them to file with the fund. The attorney general and the Immigration and Naturalization Service promised the families of undocumented workers they would not suffer any sanction or punishment by filing with the fund. INS issued a formal ruling in multiple language translations:

The Act authorizes compensation to any individual (or the personal representative of a deceased individual) who was physically injured or killed as a result of the terrorist-related aircraft crashes on September 11, 2001. It would appear, however, that some of the victims who meet that criterion do not have legal immigration status. The Department wants to assure potential claimants that their eligibility to recover under the Fund will not be affected by their nationality or immigration status.

The Department, in an effort to accomplish that purpose, will not use information that claimants submit in support of their claims under the Fund to initiate immigration proceedings against claimants who lack legal immigration status. In other words, victims and family members who entered the U.S. illegally, failed to maintain their status, or overstayed their admission, can come forward without fear that the information they provide to the Department or to the Special Master's Office will be used to initiate removal proceedings (e.g., removal from the United States, confinement, etc.). However, this assurance does not extend to those whose lack of legal immigration status is coupled with other violations of the law. For example, criminals, people who are removable on the basis of terrorist activities, and those who absconded after being ordered deported or removed can receive no such assurances.

The Department also recognizes that certain employers might be reluctant to provide helpful information to the Fund in support of an illegal immigrant's claim if such information will be used to initiate action against employers. The Department wants to assure employers that information they provided to the Fund in connection with such claims will not be used by the Government to initiate actions based on civil violations of the employer sanctions statute, pursuant to the Immigration and Nationality Act.

It is important to emphasize that this policy does not mean that aliens who are unlawfully present in the United States can never be removed or that those who are currently in lawful status cannot be removed based on future violations of the law. It does mean, however, that aliens who are unlawfully present in the United States because they have not attained or maintained lawful immigration status, and who have suffered grave loss as the result of September 11, do not need to fear that information that they submit in support of a claim under the Fund will be used by the Government to initiate immigration proceedings.

Once again, the painstaking work paid off. We managed to track down the families of the eleven undocumented workers. Those who needed green cards to stay in the United States received them, and the families received generous payments to help them resume their struggle to realize their own piece of the American Dream.

The sheer volume of documentation needed to corroborate our calculations of economic loss threatened to turn my office into a glorified accounting firm. The 9/11 statute mandated individual compensation in the millions of dollars. With such amounts at stake, it was imperative that all individual claims be well documented. This proved extremely difficult. Grieving families were overwhelmed by the paperwork. They complained (understandably) about the length of the application, the ambiguity of some questions, the intricacies of the requested facts and figures. It was all too confusing.

Applications we received were often incomplete or, even worse, inconsistent. A policeman's widow might state in the claim form that her dead husband had been earning $64,000 per year while the accompanying W2 tax form referenced only $46,000 in income. Was her husband moonlighting at a second job? Had she accurately reported the income? A stockbroker's widow might highlight the value of stock options in filing a claim, but closer examination showed that the pertinent tax returns made no mention of this income. Which was correct? Our staff had to figure it out.

Each claim required a careful parsing of facts and figures, and in some cases an executive decision that might affect many other claimants. For example, hundreds of families informed us they'd received workers compensation payments after the deaths of the victims, but that the workers compensation insurance carriers were demanding that the money be repaid out of their 9/11 awards. It would be extremely unfair, they argued, to offset such compensation when repayment was required. They had a point; I decided not to offset these contingent payments.

There was also the specter of fraud. I'd read news stories about people filing phony insurance claims at the World Trade Center and was determined to minimize the likelihood of fraud in my administration of the 9/11 fund. Was this a genuine concern? Yes. One of the first claims we received asked that any award be transferred by wire to a hotel in Panama! As you might imagine, that provoked an immediate investigation—one of several during the lifetime of the fund.

I tried to protect the fund from fraudulent claims by requiring detailed documentation and by asking the Department of Justice Fraud Division to investigate any suspicious claims that came our way. In the end, we sent only twenty-six suspicious applications to the department for investigation. Six individuals were prosecuted and convicted for fraudulent claims, ranging from the fabrication of a loved one who supposedly died on 9/11 to the faking of an eligible injury.

Unfortunately the concern about fraud meant that many applications had to be examined and reexamined. Second and third reviews became common. Delay was unavoidable, though understandably frustrating for both the families and our staff, which was struggling to handle the flood of applications in a timely fashion.

While I depended on my staff to evaluate the applications, I alone had the ultimate responsibility of determining each award, based largely on a prediction of what the victim would have earned had he or she survived. It was a job that called for the wisdom of Solomon, the technical skill of H&R Block, and the insight of a mystic with a crystal ball. I was supposed to peer into that crystal ball, consider the ebbs and flows that made up a stranger's life, and translate all of this into dollars and cents. No matter what my decision in any individual case, I was subject to second-guessing. I was accused of misreading the present and demeaning the victim's future. Uncertainty, driven by the unknown and the unknowable—the difficulty of predicting what might have been—was inherent in the very structure of the program.

"Mr. Feinberg," one mother told me in my office, "if only you had met my son and listened to him plan his future, you would have been sold on his optimism." Another widow demanded, "Why did my next-door neighbor receive $1.2 million from you, while I only got $865,000? We both were wives of policemen who made the same money and were part of the same union contract. Why are you picking on me? Don't you like me?"

The ambiguity of payments delayed individuals from entering the fund. A typical claimant on the cusp would say, "Mr. Feinberg, I might come into the fund or I might sue. How much will I get from you if I file? I want to know my options."

The questions came at a dizzying pace. Would the stockbroker have continued to earn millions? Or would the economy have gone south, and his compensation with it? Would the dishwasher, thrilled with his first job since arriving from the Dominican Republic, quickly advance up the salary scale? Or would he become a permanent member of the hidden economic underclass, tied to a subsistence salary? How much reliance should I place on the statement of a grieving mother: "My daughter had just graduated from college. She was a star and would certainly have become a major success in the business world"? Where is it written that all college graduates are guaranteed success? How does one define "success"? An annual salary of $50,000? $100,000? $1,000,000? And what could I possibly say to a mother determined to write her dead daughter's future, a future that would never be?

As the applications poured in and the families lined up at my office door, I learned more and more about the uncertainty that came with my job. At the outset, I envisioned what I called a "common law of awards" that would help applicants understand the size of awards and the objective factors I relied on in reaching my decisions. Cold reality—the infinite variations of the human condition—made this excruciatingly difficult. I tried to treat similar claims alike. But I soon learned that there were few truly "similar" claims. A minor distinction here, an additional fact there meant that the final calculations varied dramatically from claim to claim, and for good reason. The victims were all different. Their achievements, hopes, aspirations, and goals added up to five thousand different lives. Therefore I had to issue five thousand different awards. There was no way around it.

The judgment I used in calculating awards was driven, of course, not only by the statute and regulations but also by my background and values. I relied in part on my experience in resolving and administering mass tort cases like Agent Orange. But in no previous case had I been required to calculate awards based on the principle of economic loss. And in all of my other cases, a finite amount of money ($180 million in the Agent Orange case) had been made available for me to distribute to eligible claimants based upon a fixed formula: X amount for a case of cancer, X amount for emphysema, X amount for a broken arm or leg. The 9/11 statute was entirely different. There was no fixed, appropriated amount for me to distribute; I would tally the total check as I went along. And there were no fixed rules for allocation.

Judge Weinstein had urged me to distribute funds as quickly as possible and bring an efficient end to the program sooner rather than later. "The longer you stay out there, the visible symbol of 9/11, the more you become a target for families with all sorts of anger and hurt," he warned me. But as the process unfolded, I realized that being fair was more important than being fast.

Where could I look for guidance? My own life? Because of my blue-collar background and Jewish heritage, I was inclined to defend the underdog—to provide extra help to the less fortunate. But was that right? Frustrated, I met with my friend Rabbi William Hamilton of Temple Kehillath Israel, one of Boston's oldest and most respected synagogues. He explained that some of life's most complex, unfathomable mysteries had no answers— that the Jewish texts deliberately avoided providing simplistic solutions when no explanation would suffice. To Rabbi Hamilton, at least, the unique trauma of 9/11 was so unprecedented, so horrific, it was unexplainable. It was fruitless to seek ready-made answers in Scripture or the wisdom of the past.

As individual decisions accumulated, I found my choices driven by two overarching principles. First, the fund should be compassionate and generous but not profligate, dispensing taxpayers' money by the fistful. I wanted to be recognized as a wise fiduciary, a sound custodian of the taxpayers' money, lest I forfeit the bipartisan support I received in administering the program. I recalled the unfortunate experience of Representative Richard Bland Lee of Virginia, appointed by President James Madison after the War of 1812 to compensate citizens whose homes had been destroyed by occupying British troops. Lee's promising career was ruined by a public perception that he had been too generous and unprincipled in his compensation decisions. I did not want to become a similar sad footnote in American history.

Second, I used my discretion as Congress intended, as a safety valve against runaway awards and low-end payments. The law required me to make distinctions among claimants, and I personally intervened to limit high-end awards and raise depressed payments. Awarding everybody the same amount was expressly prohibited by statute, but I could narrow the gap between the wealthy, the middle-class, and the poor. And that's what I did.

Thankfully, the support I received from members of Congress never wavered. Occasionally a representative or senator would call or write on behalf of a constituent.

"Mrs. X has been in to see me," the letter might say. "She's concerned about whether she'll be treated fairly by the fund. Will you please keep an eye on her case and let me know if there's anything I can do?" Of course, I did so.

Of all the members of Congress whose constituents were massively affected by 9/11, the one I heard from the most frequently was New York Senator Hillary Rodham Clinton. I was impressed by her devotion to constituent service arising out of 9/11. As it happens, the New York office of my law firm is in the same building as her local office, and I would sometimes meet with a group of 9/11 families in one of her conference rooms.

After one such meeting, Senator Clinton offered some encouragement. "Ken, keep doing what you're doing. And remember," she added, "no good deed goes unpunished." I would remember these words throughout my tenure.

CHAPTER FOUR

The Families Speak

THOUSANDS OF 9/11 families and victims filed applications with the fund. The applicants were as varied as the relatives they had lost in the attacks—rich and poor, young and old, American citizens and foreign visitors. Some were spouses, some fiancées, and some gay domestic partners. For most, the application process was an opportunity—at long last—for the survivors of the attacks to speak their minds, express their feelings, explore the magnitude of their loss.

The irony of the entire process quickly became apparent. To receive the promised check from the United States Treasury, the applicants were compelled to wade through thirty-three pages of antiseptic bureaucratic language—name, address, social security number, compensation, offsets, sources of income, number of dependents, work life expectancy, stock options, bonuses, commissions, collateral offsets. But it was important that the claim form provide the survivors with an opportunity to paint a more three-dimensional picture of the victim. So, in part II of the claim form applicants were invited to explain what the numbers could never convey, the uniqueness of the husband, wife, daughter, son or parent. This went a long way toward tempering the claim form's reliance on cold, purely objective facts and figures.

Many wrote about the impact of their loss, the hole left by the missing loved one, how 9/11 had tragically and irreparably changed their lives. Many applicants were angry. They needed to vent, to flail away at life's misfortunes and cruelties. Here was their chance to do so.

The applications were only the beginning. Fund procedures stipulated that any applicant or interested party could also ask to visit with me in person to discuss the application process. Some asked to see me only after they received formal notification of their award. They sought what we called a Track A appeal, usually to express their unhappiness with the amount of the check. They made personal entreaties, hoping that intimate details about the victim would lead me to increase the award amount. Others arranged to see me beforehand, at so-called Track B hearings, in order to influence the amount of their award before a decision was made.

But these meetings were rarely limited to reviews of the raw data that would go into computing their awards. Instead, the applicants wanted to discuss the unquantifiable value of their lost loved one. They wanted to talk about the victim, about his commitment to family, her generosity, their heroism on 9/11. Their loved one was *different* from the others; she was unique, and this uniqueness should be reflected in the award.

And so I found myself meeting with thousands of applicants on an individual basis. I decided to make it as convenient as possible by visiting claimants in or near their homes. When I visited an elderly woman in Brooklyn who had lost her son, she gave me a tour of her home and offered me tea and pastries before explaining the magnitude of her loss and the injustice of her surviving the death of her son.

I scheduled more formal hearings in local fund offices throughout the nation. Before attending these hearings, I would review a one-page summary of the facts prepared by my staff. I then met with whoever wanted to see me, often beginning a day of hearings at 7:00 A.M. Each hearing lasted about thirty minutes, although a particularly complex hearing could run well over an hour. I set no time limit. After offering bagels, doughnuts, and coffee, I urged the family members to speak their piece.

A stenographer was present to administer an oath to all witnesses and record what was said. Nonetheless, the hearings were usually quite informal, avoiding the technicalities of the courtroom. They provided the claimant an opportunity to vent, to help me understand the victim and what the loss meant to the survivors. Claimants rarely appeared alone; they brought friends, colleagues of the victim, clergymen, accountants, economists, and, in many cases, lawyers.

(A word concerning the lawyers: About three-quarters of the 9/11 families were represented by lawyers, most of them offering their services on a pro bono basis. Many others retained legal counsel at reduced fees, generally between 8 and 10 percent of the final fund award. My fellow attorneys played an enormous role in helping thousands of victims navigate a terribly difficult time, a gesture of public service of which our profession should be very proud.)

As if feeling the inadequacy of mere words, the family members also brought physical evidence—photograph albums, scrapbooks, videos of weddings, bar mitzvahs, graduations, and life at home. They brought medals, citations, and honors that had been bestowed on the victim. Some played recordings of songs written especially to honor the death of the loved one, while others read poems and eulogies. All this in an attempt to paint a more accurate picture of the victim. My office was inundated with memorabilia, all of which became part of the official record of the proceedings. (This material was stored at PriceWaterhouseCoopers and is now in the process of being returned to the claimants.)

Nor was it just for me that families brought this memorabilia. They were visibly comforted as they slowly turned the pages of the albums for me or explained the importance of a high school graduation certificate, a first communion video, a medal for heroism. Often they would stop and reflect on a particular item, fingering it gently, lost in memory. It was as if I was not even in the room.

I would occasionally comment about a photograph or stop the video to highlight a moment, expressing interest but also demonstrating my determination to learn more about the victim, to show that I was interested in more than statistics. This was the human side of the program, an attempt to temper family perceptions that the fund was only interested in cold, hard calculations. Real people had died, and I was interested in learning more about those lives lost on 9/11.

A few applicants wanted to play voice message recordings from their spouses trapped in the upper floors of the World Trade Center on 9/11. I tried to convince them that such recordings need not be part of the public record, but most family members rejected my advice. They wanted me to hear the phone calls. An ominous hush filled the conference room as the claimant pushed "play" on the tape recorder and voices crackled to life. We sat silently, reliving the fear, horror, and desperation of those trapped in the buildings. When I asked one spouse why she would keep such a tape recording in her possession, she replied, "To bear witness to what those monsters did to my husband. I want the world to remember."

During these hearings I encountered every imaginable emotion, from despair to anger to resignation to uncontrollable grief. One day, the 9/11 hearing room would serve as a kind of psychiatrist's office, the next day as a confessional, the day after that as a forum for an impassioned debate about terrorism. On more than one occasion, it became a type of family court with arguing family members disputing each other's claim to the funds. These difficult situations placed me in the role of a psychiatrist, family counselor, grief expert, rabbi and priest—often on the same day and even during the same hearing, as the kaleidoscope of human emotions played out before my eyes.

Confronting these intense emotions was a humbling experience. How could I ever meet the expectations of the 9/11 families? How could I provide answers where no answer would suffice?

Through the 9/11 hearing process, I witnessed how human beings respond to tragedy. I saw how family members struggled to confront their loss and move on with their lives. Some couldn't; they were too overwhelmed with grief. Others were fueled by a burning anger that seemed to help them get a grip on their disrupted lives. Many families exhibited frustration with life's unfairness. "Why me?" they asked. "Why was my wife killed? She was a saint, a wonderful mother, a community leader. Why is she gone?" Others were blessed with the courage and fortitude to continue living. "I'll go on for the sake of my kids. I'll never give the murderers the satisfaction of knowing that they have beat me down." For many, religious faith was a lifeline; for others, 9/11 shattered all religious conviction.

I personally presided over 931 track A and track B hearings in less than two years, conducting as many as a dozen a day, often well into the evening. (Other lawyers on the fund staff or borrowed from various government agencies presided at more than 600 additional hearings.) Hearing after hearing hammered home the devastating impact of 9/11 on ordinary families who never anticipated the wrenching change imposed on their lives. The testimony about loss and tragedy could not help but affect me and everybody in the room. On more than one occasion, I left the building during a break between hearings and walked around the block to clear my head and prepare myself for the next family. These days were emotionally and physically exhausting, but I soldiered on, determined to give each family its due.

A cynic might say that the hearings were all about money, that the emotional outpourings were well-orchestrated attempts to win greater cash payments. Maybe so—in a few cases. But the testimonials and memorabilia also helped many claimants gain some degree of psychological closure. In order to move on with their own lives, they first had to lay bare the life that ended on 9/11. And they had to perform this exorcism in front of someone. I happened to be there as a government representative to witness and preside over these final reflections and good-byes. They would move on. But first, the memories of their lost loved ones needed to be memorialized in an official proceeding.

Of course, many claimants did not use the 9/11 fund as an outlet for their feelings. Thousands simply filed applications and never requested hearings. Administering the fund taught me just how varied is the human response to tragedy. Some take solace in publicly sharing their innermost emotions; others would never dream of exposing their emotions to outsiders. While some would discuss 9/11 with anybody within listening range, I knew that others remained in their homes behind locked doors, unable to confront the world. On the anniversary of 9/11, some families involved themselves intensely in the public ceremonies at the World Trade Center, the Pentagon, and Shanksville, Pennsylvania. They lit candles and helped read aloud the names of the dead. Other made a conscious decision to avoid recognizing the anniversary date. They did not turn on the television that day or read a newspaper. Who is to say which path is the better one?

The stories I heard during the fund hearings open a window into the minds of the survivors. They demonstrate how human beings confront the horror of sudden tragedy and loss. In this sense, the 9/11 families teach us valuable lessons about human nature under life's most extreme stress.

Anger was the primary response of many families and surviving victims, often fueled by their conviction that the tragedy could and should have been averted, and that retribution should be visited on the murderers. For these families, there was little time for grief or even quiet reflection. There was too much important work to be done in bringing the murderers to justice and allocating responsibility for the tragedy here at home. In their applications, these families expressed the raw anger they felt and their desire for vengeance. One widow eloquently described the passion behind her decision to enter the fund:

I am forfeiting my right to sue even though I know my husband's death could have and should have been prevented.

I am forfeiting my right to sue despite my desire to punish and hold accountable all those that I feel are responsible for my husband's death.

But this does not mean that I do not want to sue.

I want to sue the foreign governments that harbor and support terrorist organizations.

I want to sue our government, who despite their claims of ignorance, had warnings that terrorists were going to strike us in the manner and on the scale in which they did.

I want to sue the airlines, which, through the simplest of security measures, could have prevented the hijacking that led to my husband's death.

I want to sue the architects and the builders of the World Trade Center, who constructed buildings that did not even meet New York City Building Codes, buildings that were so flawed in their design and structure that they crumbled to dust as the world watched.

I want to sue the government of this city for continuing to send its civil servants into what was obviously a terrorist attack and not an accident.

I want to sue the Fire Department, whose leaders

continued to send their members into what experience and common sense should have told them was a
hopeless situation.

But my desire to hold accountable those that are
responsible for the tragedy of 9/11 is outweighed by
the needs of my children. My children and I must put
this behind us and go on with our lives.

Many applicants focused their intense anger on the
perpetrators of 9/11, in particular the terrorist master-
mind, Osama bin Laden. One spouse stated:

> If you speak to the president, I want to see bin
> Laden's head on a plate, just like Salome in the
> opera... I think that should be the major objective of
> our country... and I want his head. I want him dead,
> and everybody else connected out of this country. No
> more immigrants except the people that we know
> should be coming here. And that's what I want more
> than your award or the government's sympathy.

We tend to think of anger as a negative, destructive
force. But this kind of anger got many of these families
out of bed in the morning and fueled their determination
to get through the day. They had no time to be depressed.
They had business to take care of—vengeance to seek.
Perhaps, for these families, anger was a way of embracing
life again.

Of course, the 9/11 fund wasn't responsible for measuring the culpability of our government. When families in private or public sessions would spend an inordinate amount of time denouncing the government for failing to prevent the attacks, I would eventually interrupt and say, "If you're angry at the government for not preventing the attacks, you've come to the wrong forum. I suggest you speak to the 9/11 Commission and the House and Senate Intelligence Committees. What we are doing here is beyond politics—a pure program to help people."

And indeed, many of the 9/11 families did appear before those other forums and helped influence the public debate over the most effective ways to combat terrorism. In the process, they helped divert public attention away from my work with the fund and toward other issues of importance for the future of our nation. For example, the famous Jersey Girls—Kristin Breitweiser, Patty Casazza, Lorie Van Auken, and Mindy Kleinberg—four young women who lost husbands on 9/11, spent a great amount of time and energy in the early months of the fund program publically questioning the regulations and procedures we established. But within a few months, they shifted their focus to the larger national debate and made a lasting contribution.

Of course, the 9/11 families did not limit their anger to the terrorists or others they deemed responsible for the attacks. Many families expressed outrage at the failure of the authorities to find the bodies of their loved ones so that they could bury and honor them at funeral services. (The search process lasted for years. In February 2005, the New York City medical examiner concluded that, after exhaustive investigation and testing, no identification could be made of over 1,100 victims who died at the World Trade Center.) This focus on human remains was either the result of religious conviction or simply the need to confront death in a final chapter involving the physical burial of the victim. I was surprised by the angry emotional outbursts of family members unable to find psychological closure without the burial of their loved ones. Anger became the dominant emotion when no body was recovered. Seemingly the horror and death associated with 9/11 were compounded by the absence of a body.

One mother wrote:

> All my available time now is spent trying to ensure a proper burial for my son and those who died with him. Instead, he lies with the trash at the Fresh Kills Landfill. . . .
>
> Another Mother's Day is approaching, and I know I cannot even visit his gravesite. And every day I awake knowing that my son's cemetery is a garbage dump, and I can't stand it.

Some family members went beyond personal expressions of anger and actually established an organization, WTC Families for Proper Burial, to make sure that the authorities would not cover the Fresh Kills landfill and other areas where physical remains might yet be found. These families often used the 9/11 fund application process

to express their outrage. One such family member lashed
out at the unfairness of a son disappearing without a trace:

> I'm angry. I'm angry. I have to be honest, I'm angry
> with our country also, because they let this happen.
> My beautiful boy was cremated because of them. I
> never got anything back ...
>
> If somebody took your child and blew them up
> and you didn't have a piece of a fingernail left, how
> do you live from—how do you go on from there? I'll
> never be the same.

Sadly, some family members also directed their anger
toward each other. The fund became a forum for battles
among family members and friends, each demanding
their fair share of award money. This family squabbling
often led to angry denunciations of "unworthy" members
who had no right to become wealthy at the expense of
the victim. Each party was convinced it was fighting in
memory of the victim who would not, could not, be sul-
lied through inappropriate awards to the undeserving.
And so parents squared off against children and spouses
fought with parents.

I reviewed many ugly tales of family bickering, fueled by anger and resentment, such as these from a grand-
parent:

> Let's talk about the two girls first.
> They're angry. They are very angry at their mother.

They don't want to speak to her. They don't want to see her. But I can't keep them from her by law, so when she calls to ask for a visitation, I comply always. And whenever she calls the house, I give the phone to the children.

The children—every single time [the mother] is on the phone, she says, "I would love you guys to call me; here's my number." The children have never called her. I've suggested they call her. They don't want to call her. They don't want any contact with her.

It would have been futile for me to insert myself into these family feuds. I could not cool such passions by urging reason and calmness. Besides, I was the administrator of a government program, not a family counselor. Much of this family squabbling had been seething for years, with decades of slights now drawn to the surface by tragedy. Where did the truth lie? I rarely took sides, seeking to avoid alienating family members who would then question my objectivity. Instead, I tried to remain above the fray. I urged compromise and threatened to withhold awards until and unless family peace was achieved. This threat usually worked An uneasy peace would prevail, and the award would be issued and distributed among competing claimants based on the agreement I helped mediate. What happened after that, I do not know.

Above all, I learned to never ever use phrases like, "I stand in your shoes," or "I know what you must be experiencing." This kind of language is trite and condescending; it's also simply false. Even if I conducted 10,000 hearings, I could never begin to fathom the anger, horror, and grief these families confronted each day. I could empathize, but I could never enter their intimate personal inner sanctum of anger and sorrow. This was reserved for the chosen few, as expressed by a father mourning for his child:

> One of the worst sayings I found is when you go to a function like the Knights of Columbus or something like that and somebody says, I know what you are going through. I look at them and say, you know what I'm going through? Do you see a man without a heart? These sons of bitches ripped my heart out. I would like to get a hold of them and explain things because this kid meant so much to me. It is unbelievable. Nobody can say I know what you are going through. One thing. I would like to preach to people, don't say that to anybody. Don't say I know what you are going through unless you are going through it. Unless you are sitting in our shoes. You can't say I know what you are going through. It is a tough thing. There's no such thing as I know what you are going through.

Grief, of course, usually dominated the atmosphere of the hearings, pervasive and unyielding. Tears flowed freely. I often had to interrupt a hearing so that family members, friends and acquaintances could compose themselves or attempt to do so. On more than one occasion, a matter-of-fact hearing involving the calculation of economic loss, or a discussion of which family members were entitled to an award, would come to an abrupt halt because of a chance comment about the victim—her role as a mother, his dreams about the future. We would all sit there, staring at the gaping human vacuum created by an untimely and totally unexpected death.

One wife told me of the traumatic events surrounding the discovery of her husband's body:

> My son wants to go to the graveyard and dig him up, and I'm like, "We can't dig up Daddy." I haven't told him they're still finding daddy.
>
> They found his upper torso first, and they asked me if he was wearing his wedding ring. And I said "No, why?" "Because he was missing his left hand."
>
> And since then they found his right leg and right ankle. There's still pieces of him in the city.

The misidentification of bodies led to bizarre situations. Considering the nature of the tragedy and the massive loss of life, it was not surprising that bodies were misidentified and official errors made in notifying survivors about remains that were often disfigured beyond recognition. Indeed, it is surprising that there were not more incidents of misidentification—a tribute to the mili-

tary and civilian medical examiners and to the evolving
science of DNA identification.

Nevertheless, at least two hearings revealed how
misidentification compounded family grief.

They finally found [him]. They brought [his] remains
home. They had a big funeral service, memorial, and
they buried [him].

Three months later, they found that they hadn't
buried [him]. It was the wrong individual that they
had been provided the remains of.

They had to disinter and give to the family the
proper remains and then bury [him] again.

The second case was even more heart wrenching.
Because of misidentification, family members were
unaware that their husband and father had actually survived the terrorist attacks at the World Trade Center and
had been hospitalized in New York City for four days
before dying. The wife of the victim sobbed during the
hearing as she described the agony of lost time:

I was furious because they robbed me of the time that I
could have spent with him. I found out that he lived
days after that terrible accident, and that time we could
have sat by his side and prayed along with him because
there's a chance that he could have heard us and pulled
through, but we were just robbed of the moment.

Instead, a *second* family had conducted this bedside vigil, erroneously believing the victim in the hospital bed was their loved one. They then buried the victim only to be informed later about the misidentification. The sister of the victim described the family's ordeal:

> We were told that because he suffered about 90 percent burns over his body, he would be bandaged up and he would be under wraps and he might not appear to be the same person that we know him to be.
>
> We went in there and thought this was the person, because his name was with the, his name was on the bed. We stayed with him pretty much until the night of the 15th, when we got a call in the middle of the night saying that he went into a third respiratory arrest. We rushed back to the hospital and it was already too late. We held services for him on the 22nd.
>
> And then on the 24th, got a call from the Medical Examiner's Office saying that, that, that there was a mix-up, when they brought in the, the two people, and, and we had to make another identification.
>
> But we—we did this, and after identifying him, we decided to hold a second ceremony for my brother, but not tell my parents, because they were not in a state to receive it, added to the fact that aside from my brother, my niece was also lost in the attack. So I didn't think that my parents could have been in, could have handled it mentally.

So, so we held the second ceremony after disinterring the body, bringing him back, actually bringing him to the burial site, performing services again ... [The] headstone has no date on it, because [my] parents believe that he passed away on the 15th, when in fact, he passed away on the 11th.... The family spent four days [at the hospital] with another person.

As this story unfolded, the initial calm of the proceedings was interrupted by gasps and sobs. The entire atmosphere of the hearing was transformed, as if a tornado had suddenly touched down in the hearing room. I adjourned the hearings and invited the witnesses to compose themselves in an adjourning room. I welcomed the opportunity to get my bearings as well. I needed an adjournment. Although I was determined to maintain an official atmosphere at the hearings, to exhibit the cool understanding of a professional, there were limits to this personal detachment. When reality became stranger than fiction, it was time to take a break. A few minutes later, once the families had composed themselves, we started up again.

This kind of emotional upheaval happened frequently. I could never predict when this shift might occur, at the beginning of the hearing, in the middle, or at the end. But I learned to anticipate early signs of intense grief—the pregnant pause, the quivering lip, the deep sigh, the hands covering the face. I felt conflicted in such situations. I encouraged those in the hearing room to express their feelings and to articulate the full range of their emotions. I informed them that I welcomed any and all information that would help me better understand the life that was lost. But I also wanted to avoid emotional scenes that would disrupt the hearings and add an additional layer of grief or embarrassment.

Sometimes, in an effort to forestall a gathering emotional storm, I would ask irrelevant questions and attempt to divert the attention of those about to falter. My goal was to alter the atmosphere in the room, to lance the emotional intensity of the moment. Usually my strategy worked, but occasionally it didn't and the hearing broke down.

Disconsolate claimants often wanted to explain the role of grief in their daily lives, how it impacted them and affected their ability to get through the day. While some lamented life's unfairness, others recognized that grief and joy were part of the same equation, an emotional calculation that made up a life:

> She taught me to realize that every day is a choice to be happy or not.
>
> She taught me to be present in each moment. And they aren't all happy, like today. They aren't all meant to be. But sadness is as much a part of life as joy, and so the sadness that I feel at losing her is almost equivalent to the joy that she shared with me while she was alive.
>
> So those to me are some very big lessons, and I hope that's the right way to answer the little question of who was [the victim].

Many families forced themselves to focus on memories of happier days. Memory was their inner strength, a means to channel grief in a positive direction. It helped them get out of bed each morning and move on with life. The hearings repeatedly demonstrated the crucial importance of memory in assuaging grief. Memory reinforced resolve, even when the witness appeared devastated. In the emotional wreckage following 9/11, memories of happier times provided a valuable link between the old world and the new.

But some claimants could not get past their loss. Their grief was too fresh, dominating all else. The stark reality of personal loss ruled the day:

> [He's] gone forever. I can't believe it. I won't believe it.
>
> How does one go on from here? Every waking day you're hit with a sledgehammer to the heart, reminding you that the world you knew pre–9/11 will never ever be again the same...
>
> So I ask you, how has my life changed?
>
> If I cut off one of your legs, you'd still walk, but not as well. So here I am this one-legged man, trying to cope in a world that harbors hateful, demonic people who would drive a plane through a building, taking the lives of almost 3,000 individuals.

Was any of the grief staged for my benefit? Perhaps a little. I like to think I became rather expert in discerning the real emotions from the disingenuous. On two occasions—a spouse who only learned of her husband's infidelity after his death, and a child angry that her dead mother had deserted the family years earlier—I discerned the clear implication that the victim was more valuable in death than he or she had been in life. But such cases were rare.

Most claimants expressed a deep, enduring love for the lost victim. There was anger and grief, but love was also a prevailing emotion in the hearing room.

Claimants offered up capsule versions of family lives full of love—parents playing with children, husbands and wives sharing life's happy and sad moments, grandparents glowing at the accomplishments of grandchildren, lovers planning their bright and promising futures. All of these stories were bound together by love.

It was obviously impossible to verify all such stories. There was no test we could use to determine the legitimacy and credibility of such assertions. How could I even begin to challenge claims of love and loss? And why bother? What purpose would be served?

Why did the families want so desperately to paint vivid pictures of love and of hopes now dashed? It wasn't about the money. It was a deep, internal need to find psychological closure by sharing such emotions as part of an official record. In a few cases, when I believed this search for closure was especially acute—when the sobbing family members commented that they had very little tangible evidence by which to remember the victim—I would invite them to obtain a copy of the hearing transcript and place it in a safe deposit box as a type of memorial so that future generations could read about the overwhelming love that bound survivors to the memory of those lost. In this concrete way, undying love would survive the passing of generations.

I was hardest hit by the love and devotion of parents saying good-bye to children. One mother poured out her heart in describing what the death of her son meant to her, that you had to be a parent to appreciate the magnitude of the loss:

There is no greater love than the unconditional love between a parent and a child.... When he would be out late at night, I couldn't sleep. Then I would hear him park his car and climb into the basement window. What a great feeling to know he was home. It takes a parent to know that feeling.... I think of him when we see his friends getting married and having children. I miss him when I see mothers, fathers and children together, and then I think our family has one child missing.... My son... meant the world to me. He'll always be my little boy. I miss him more than words can ever say. He was one of the greatest joys of my life, and I'll always love him.

Expressions of love were particularly intense among surviving widows who were pregnant on 9/11 and now came to the hearings with children who would never know their father. There were over sixty of these young widows. They spoke of the cruel unfairness of life and of the love between father and child that would never be:

> The loss is not the greatest for me; I had five years with [my husband]...I remember having so many dreams where he would come and take [our son] from me and [my husband] would say "Just give me five minutes. I just need five minutes and I'll give him back." And if I could give him five minutes, I'd give him five minutes, because he never had anything.

Such testimonies provided me with a new perspective, a new appreciation for the powerful impact of love on the day-to-day experiences of family members whose lives were forever altered on 9/11. Love proved to be a powerful force among 9/11 families. It bound families together. It reinforced bonds that may have been frayed by the tragedy. It became obvious to all of us working on the fund that love was often all that survivors could cling to—a life preserver—in their effort to get through each day. They had been left behind, but they had been left behind with powerful reserves of love. This love could reinforce their resolve, provide them a compass for living. It could give them a reason for moving on.

When I was a young child in Brockton, Massachusetts, my mother told me that "tears are the price of love." Decades later, I witnessed firsthand how grief and love were woven together and how love could overcome the most formidable of obstacles. During the hearings, expressions of love seemed to trump all other human emotions, including fear, grief, and anger at the crimes committed. These stories of love often helped me through the day, when hearing after hearing stretched late into the night.

At times, I doubted the wisdom of this approach. Were the hearings such a good idea? Why not just issue the awards on the basis of the claim forms and supporting documentation? Why dredge up all this emotion and place it on display in the hearing room? But when I wavered in my thinking, a family would enter the hearing room and express a love toward the victim so overwhelming and selfless it renewed my faith and determination to carry on.

I went home at night and hugged my wife and children with a new intensity, ready to conduct more hearings the next day.

CHAPTER FIVE

Struggling with the Incomprehensible

IF GRIEF, anger, and love were the dominant reactions to the 9/11 attacks, close behind came fear.

Some families were so traumatized by 9/11 that they continued to live in fear—fear of another terrorist attack, fear that they were no longer safe, fear that any type of public announcement about their award could lead to the kidnapping of their children. A few families refused to attend 9/11 hearings unless they were conducted on lower floors or in the basement of the building housing my offices. Some families refused to travel to New York City for the hearings. They were convinced that the bridges into Manhattan were imminent terrorist targets or that fate would dictate a terrorist attack on the very day that they visited New York City. They warned me of the dangers lurking in city streets and neighborhoods. Fear had become the driving force in their lives, an emotion that overshadowed all others and that affected their day-to-day decisions—when to get up in the morning and when to run the risk of visiting the supermarket or the doctor's office.

Some felt that the 9/11 attacks were the prelude for another major act of violence directed at America. We were all living on borrowed time. Nothing I could say or do could diminish their sense of foreboding. Fear controlled their lives, a fear bordering on paranoia: "As we speak, we're an endangered species in this country," one widow told me. "Because looking over your shoulder, they're all out there, and they're ready to take down the next set of buildings. And I live with that."

This post–9/11 obsession with security and worry about the future forced some families to make major lifestyle changes in order to lessen the likelihood that they would once again be the victims of a second terrorist attack. Since the U.S. government could no longer protect them, and since the terrorists were living in their own neighborhoods waiting for the right moment to strike again, escape was the only option available. But was any place safe? Could they ever get far enough from New York City or Washington? Even the tiniest rural village in deepest America could be unsafe. For some, the paranoia was paralyzing:

> I feel we're in great danger. I forced my husband to leave New York, and [my daughter]. I've been begging them for two years. I forced them. Finally, [my daughter] left two weeks ago, and she's in ... [Long Island] ...

And my husband, he doesn't want to leave New York, but my life is too terror stricken with everything that's going on. I am in dire fear for the whole city, and our life has changed this way. I want to just pack up everybody and go. But where? Where am I going to go?

Fear also preyed on families who looked back at the days before 9/11. They remembered how worried some loved ones had been about working in the World Trade Center, as if they'd had a premonition of 9/11. During the hearings, family members would testify about this fear, explaining that they just *knew* the attacks would occur, sooner or later, and that the victim knew it as well, that they had talked about it. The witnesses would stare at me with this "I knew it all the time" look. The events of 9/11 should have surprised nobody, they said. The attacks simply confirmed what everybody, especially our government, should have known. This attitude was particularly prevalent among families who lived through the 1993 World Trade Center bombing:

I counseled [him] at that time, in light of the '93 bombing, his understandably adverse reaction to it... [He] hated the World Trade Center and was only going back there for guaranteed earnings... and you know the building sways on top, so not only would he have a fear, he was a little paranoid, but he also would be physically nauseous in there each day.

It was a disgusting building. There was no air. It was very unclean. The bathrooms were disgusting. The office was very unkempt. You had to take three elevators to get to the top.

He'd had sinus infections from the lack of circulation and the air quality being so poor.

There was nothing appealing about the office, the building itself. . . . He hated that building, hated that building, and he would not go back if it wasn't for his family.

To these families, there was an inevitability about the attacks. They felt that 9/11 was an evil that could not have been prevented or avoided through any type of human intervention. They felt that we Americans were being toyed with by unexplained forces. There was no escape. The future was filled with gloom. The dark side had won:

> We never liked her working in the World Trade Center. I guess I'm just pessimistic by nature . . . My concern was always terrorism. We would talk about it and she'd say, "Oh, if you're going to die, you're going to die, so you can't worry about it."
>
> I'm glad we actually talked about it, because we actually did discuss what would happen if something happened.
>
> But, yeah, the concern was terrorism, and unfortunately it proved to be correct.

*

But the flip side of fear is courage. And I heard incredible stories of courage from 9/11 fund applicants. Some focused on the bravery of those who lost their lives attempting to help others escape from the World Trade Center and the Pentagon; they explained with pride how a husband or wife, son or daughter, had stayed behind in order to lead others to safety, only to miss the last elevator or to find the last escape route blocked. Stories of heroism and sacrifice were often told in vivid detail:

So the elevators came, and everybody piled on and there wasn't room for everybody. And so [my husband], being the gentleman that he was, he said, "That's okay, everyone, you go ahead." And there were two other women who weren't ready, so he said, "I'll wait with them." So everyone got out, and then another elevator never came.

And I know part of the story because he called me when they were trapped just to say that he loved me and the children, and he said—he told me he was trapped and he was having difficulty breathing.

And I was trying to be really supportive and I said, "Maybe you can get chairs." He said, "The ground is too hot to walk on." So I said, "Maybe you can get tables or something so you can get a pathway to get over to the stairs." He said, "I've tried, that's not working."

And I could hear the women screaming in the background that they didn't want to die. And he said they had plenty of water, and he heard an announce-ment—they started announcing, "Please evacuate the building." And [he] was such a—he always main-tained a sense of humor, and while he was talking to me, he was actually able to laugh at the announce-ment, and he was joking to me, saying, "I think I know I have to get out of the building."

He called 911, and I said, "I'll try and do what I can for you." And he said, "I have to go now because I can't talk anymore because I'm having trouble with air." Then that was the last I heard from him.... I got a letter from someone that worked for him, just say-ing how brave [he] had been and that he had stepped back to let other people go before him.

Similar stories confirmed that it was not just the fire-fighters and police officers who showed immense courage on 9/11, but also the stockbrokers, secretaries, bankers, and receptionists:

My wife called and I said, "Well, thank God, thank God, you are okay." She said, "Well, no, I am not." As HR Director, she was, she basically took the responsibility to make sure that everybody got out. ... She had made a 911 call two minutes before the building fell, saying there are eight people up here and, you know, we need to get down. She was still doing her job.

Many witnesses maintained that selfless acts of heroism by those who died should be rewarded with increased compensation, that the nation should recognize such acts of bravery in the calculation of awards. This was not unseemly or crass. But I refused to increase awards for acts of heroism, even if those acts were corroborated and well documented. To do so would force me to make distinctions about degrees of heroism, which would simply fuel divisiveness among families. My goal was to minimize distinctions among claimants, not maximize them. Heroism by all was presumed.

Physical injury victims told their own courageous stories of survival, recounting how they miraculously made it out of the buildings despite broken bones and burned flesh. The total number of very seriously injured victims—survivors who had suffered broken bodies and almost fatal burns—was, fortunately, well below expectations. In such relatively rare cases, it was possible to document, in an objective fashion, their pain, suffering, and determination to survive. I listened to their firsthand accounts of the tragedy and subsequent hospitalization. I also received testimony from their attending physicians and family members who maintained bedside vigils, often for many months. The victims themselves recounted in excruciating detail the story of their broken lives after 9/11, their near-death experiences, and their determination to survive. Such courage would be compensated:

My therapists will tell you that I am the toughest person they have ever met.

Not only have I had to live through near mortal wounds, but I continue to push myself to get better, and I never stop trying. I'm a perfectionist in many ways. And as much as it's been helpful in my recovery, because I never quit trying, it is also detrimental, because I am rarely content or satisfied with my efforts....

I hope to be normal one day. To me, that means walking down the streets of Manhattan in a crowd and no one could pick me out for being different. Believing it is possible has power, so I believe with all my heart....

I am a fighter, and I intend to keep on fighting for quality of life. I intend to get to a place where I can thrive, not just survive.

And if you didn't know any of this except for my medical records, before you is a 32-year-old female who is disfigured, handicapped, brain damaged, emotionally depressed.... But I hope that you can see I am so much more than that. I am a survivor.

Another victim, David Bernard, was walking in the vicinity of the World Trade Center when he was struck by debris. Critically injured, he lingered near death for more than three months in hospitals in New York City and Boston before succumbing to his injuries. His wife, Nancy, kept a diary during these months, a type of therapy for her and her family, documenting her husband's courage and determination. She e-mailed her daily entries to friends and family to keep them abreast of David's progress. Nancy submitted her journal at the hearing and testified how her husband, despite devastating injuries, fought bravely to survive for such a long time. Increased compensation would be awarded for this type of suffering, this determination to survive:

He was paralyzed from the waist down and had extensive injuries... he was intubated, he was totally unconscious. And the doctors told us he would never walk again. He had two punctured lungs. I think he had 12 broken ribs. He had a sizeable burn on his chest. Broken hand, broken foot... The second day he awoke, and, you know, from then on, he was awake and aware.... He was a competitor. He never stopped moving. He loved life, he loved, he loved everything, you know, he loved his sports. And you got to know this to know what hell he went through... He was always going to survive. Again, it was never a question, he was going to survive. He was a competitor, he would make it... He told me two days before he died that he was going to die... the doctors would often call him Superman, because he just—they couldn't believe—he was a competitor. And we kept telling him, you know, you could do this, this is your biggest battle. And he fought, he fought so long.

I read Nancy's entire journal, her day-by-day account of her husband's struggle to survive. Emotions swirl throughout; some days are filled with hope, others despair, but there is always a sense that David will somehow overcome his injuries. A certain fatalism characterizes the diary, a sense that only David's courage will enable him to survive. The last two entries of Nancy's journal complete the story:

Day 91 December 10, 2001

It is 1:00 A.M. and I just got home from a very, very difficult night.

Late this afternoon Dave's condition started to deteriorate and his status became very unstable, due to pneumonia and other complications. They managed to get him comfortable enough for me and the kids to leave, but he is one very sick person. The next couple of days are going to be very critical, please keep him in your prayers.

Day 92 December 11, 2001

It is with great sadness that I have to write this email.

At 6:40 this evening, exactly three months from September 11th, Dave, surrounded by his family, passed away.

Thank you for all the prayers and love, we were lucky to have Dave with us for an additional three months. His poor body was just not able to fight any longer. I will follow with any arrangements at a later date.

Stories of courage were not limited to those who died or suffered physical injuries. There was also the courage of those left behind, the surviving parents, widows, and children who pressed on despite their loss. This was a different type of courage, defined by notions of self-sufficiency and a determination to care for surviving family members. Though their lives were forever altered on 9/11, witness after witness exhibited a quiet determination to make a new life, thereby vindicating in some way the importance and impact of a lost loved one. This too took great courage.

I heard many survivors say "I must move on," or "My wife would want me to do this." These ordinary citizens, who never before had to exercise any real degree of courage, were now forced by events to rally their emotions and channel their energies in a concerted effort to move on. And they would do so quietly, each in his or her own way, outside of the public eye. The cumulative impact of these individual stories had a profound effect on me. I was witnessing not just one family marshaling the necessary forces to continue living, but hundreds of families each independently rallying around the memory of a lost family member.

Seeing this happen had a special meaning for me. Knowing that 9/11 compensation contributed to each family's resolve, I renewed my efforts to validate the work of the fund. The testimony of individuals like Nancy Bernard strengthened me; I would not be adversely affected by family members who criticized me or attacked the fund. Thousands of people like Nancy were looking to the fund for assistance in moving on with their shattered lives. I would not let them down.

On more than one occasion, a survivor expressed his or her determination to get on with life as a direct response to the terrorists themselves. The terrorists could not and would not win:

> I'll tell you what, I can understand why people commit suicide. I can understand it very easy. It's the easy way out.
>
> And I'll tell you what. You know, people say you have children. But I have to be honest, it didn't matter. I won't give the bastards the satisfaction of taking another life. And for [him], I have to go on. And I have to go on for my children.

I was struck by the number of claimants who expressed this determination to prevail against the terrorists. Their reactions to the terrorists were deeply personal. It was as if the terrorists were sitting there in the room listening to the families testify. This was no longer a battle between the government in Washington and bin Laden and his al Qaeda followers. It had become an intimate showdown between the murderers and the survivors. The survivors told me that they would try to push forward, not only because the victims would want this but because doing so sent a courageous, defiant message to those responsible for 9/11.

This too was as a form of courage. The terrorists may have killed thousands, but they would not compound the tragedy by demoralizing the survivors.

Perhaps the most challenging aspect of the 9/11 fund hearings involved questions about the role of God in people's lives. In hearing after hearing, grieving family members discussed the role of faith in their lives and in the life of the victim. For some, their faith and trust in God was reaffirmed by the 9/11 tragedy; for others, the very fact of 9/11 was proof positive that God did not exist. Some blamed God for permitting the attacks, while others scoffed at the notion that God could be held responsible for the murderous acts of human beings here on earth. Some witnesses were comforted by the fact that the victim was now in the arms of God, in a better place; others lamented that the victim had been vaporized in the rubble of the attacks, had vanished without a physical trace.

More than a few families cited their faith and trust in God as the foundation for moving on with their lives. One surviving spouse testified that, as a result of 9/11 and the death of her husband, she planned to attend divinity school as "a calling... because my faith is really what has got me through the past two and a half years." Others viewed such trust as misplaced and naive. To them, a black void now existed. They felt as if they were in free fall, cut loose from any reliance on a higher being. They would go it alone.

When it came to the subject of faith, I learned a valuable lesson—that the role of religion can be described in a thousand different ways, that the faith embraced by the survivors was limited only by their individual circumstances, personalities, and characteristics. Other human emotions—anger, grief, fear—had a certain symmetry to them; victims responded in predictable ways. Not so with religion.

Many families used the 9/11 hearings as an opportunity to reaffirm their faith in God. They were convinced that their loved one had died in God's hands. God was not to blame for the horror:

> And being a Catholic, and a devout Catholic, I just said, "You know what, Jesus had the last word here." And it's not right, because I don't think Jesus handpicked [my husband] that day, even though people say the minute you're born is the minute—you know. I just think [he] was in the wrong place at the wrong time.

These families took comfort in the belief that, although the victim had been "in the wrong place at the wrong time," God would provide a better resting place: "I feel he's in a better place, and that's what I hope, and that's what kind of gives me some kind of comfort is they say he's in a better place, and I look to that," said one father. This reliance on a "better place" became the defining attitude of many at the hearings, a conviction that, despite the horror of the moment, the victim was now at peace. It allowed survivors to move on with their own lives.

Some believed that the victim was not just "in a better place" but actually present, unseen but available and observing life here on earth:

> I have a very strong faith, and he's always around me, so that helps me as well . . . because there are people that believe dead is dead, gone is gone. I don't believe that. I believe he's here right now with me, and I believe he walks with me every step of the way, and that gives me strength. But he was such an incredibly strong person in what he did, not only on that day, but in his life, that I owe it to him to try and be as strong as I can as well.

Many of these families also believed that they would eventually be united with their loved one in the afterlife. This gave them comfort:

> I know you're in a better place than this world. One day I will meet you on the other side.
>
> It's a little hard around the house without you around, but your spirit is very much alive around here.
>
> You keep smiling and looking down upon us. I know that you are in heaven and with the Lord.

Others were convinced—absolutely convinced—that the victim had perished comforted by an unyielding faith. This view, emphasizing the victim's trust in God when confronted with imminent death, helped the families carry on here on earth:

> I think that to any parent my son was the perfect son. He was. He made us proud. The only consolation I have is that at that moment he knew God and he had God in his heart and because he practiced what he learned as a child in church and he was always helping people.

I often had difficulty relating to these families' intense faith. I certainly did not question or minimize the depth of their feelings. In fact, I encouraged any expression of religious belief that would provide some comfort to grieving families. But my Jewish faith and heritage didn't embrace the notion that the spirit of the dead physically remained here on earth. Of course, I remained silent. All that mattered was that faith offer solace to the survivors.

I was more at home with those witnesses whose religious beliefs emphasized the memory of the victim. These families believed, as I do, that the good deeds of the dead are not forgotten and guide the day-to-day conduct of those left behind. The body might have disappeared on the morning of 9/11, but the impact of that life as a lesson for the living was captured forever by memory.

This particular approach to the question of life and

death is one that gave me personal solace. While I was working for the 9/11 fund, I would often start my day by reading and rereading a favorite passage from Boris Pasternak's classic novel *Dr. Zhivago*. In this scene, the title character, Yura Zhivago, comforts the critically ill Anna Ivanova with an explanation of how the memory of those departed can encourage those left behind:

> So what will happen to your consciousness? *Your* consciousness, yours, not anyone else's. Well, what are *you?*...However far back you go in your memory, it is always in some external, active manifestation of yourself that you come across your identity—in the work of your hands, in your family, in other people. And now listen carefully. You in others—this is your soul. This is what you are. This is what your consciousness has breathed and lived on and enjoyed throughout your life—your soul, your immortality, your life in others. And what now? You have always been in others and you will remain in others. And what does it matter to you if later on that is called your memory. This will be you—the you that enters the future and becomes a part of it.

I think our hearings helped nurture memories of loved ones for countless 9/11 families. In that sense, we may have helped save many souls who might otherwise have been lost.

Religion also played a crucial role in the lives of victims who were injured on 9/11. In case after case, these individuals and their doctors commented on the role faith played in reinforcing the will to live. Even when doctors saw little hope or likelihood that victims could overcome horrible injuries, faith saw them through. One doctor who treated a severe burn victim testified about this role of faith in healing:

> [The victim] was up against an impossible task to get back to 100 percent, but he certainly has made what he has made well above and beyond what most of my patients achieve. And that I think is a tribute to [him], his inner self, his wife and family support, and certainly his faith, which has many times been a statement that he has made, and with the parenthetic always by him that he gives me credit with getting his skin back on, but he gives God the credit for getting him back to himself...
>
> The best way and the quickest way to make somebody crazy, I think, is to send them to a psychiatrist, and I refuse to do that because I've got a man here who I think is functioning at a very, very high level, who has his faith, who has again and again demonstrated that he's got it all together and that he's working as hard as he has, and he's not going to stop doing that, I think, for the rest of his life.

In another case, a Navy officer at the Pentagon explained how God had prevented a burn victim from dying. When the victim was placed in the ambulance, he seemed to be breathing normally. On the spur of the moment, the officer grabbed an oxygen tank that he saw at the scene and placed it in the ambulance. During the ride to the hospital, the victim's burned lungs suddenly stopped functioning. The oxygen tank saved his life. The officer described the experience:

> [The oxygen tank] was standing up in the corner as we started to go out, and I saw the bottle sitting there, and, you know, I'm a religious person, and I'm telling you, God said, "Grab that bottle." And I grabbed it, and I just laid it on his—right on—between his legs. I had no idea if we would need that bottle for any reason. I have no reason—no idea why I grabbed it. I just did. And, in the end, in the ambulance, I found out why.

Competing attitudes about faith and religion were expressed at the hearings. Some families were convinced that there is no God. Whatever faith they had once embraced was dashed in the rubble of the World Trade Center, the Pentagon, and the airliners. Embittered by the tragedy, these witnesses angrily denounced religion, defiantly proclaiming that it would no longer play any role in their lives. Why believe in a supreme being? Why live according to the guiding principles of faith and spiritual fulfillment, when the horror and tragedy of 9/11—the randomness of death—had become such a stark reality?

These family members could not justify faith and religion. September 11 had changed everything.

Surviving spouses testified about the difficulties in explaining the tragedy to young children who wanted to know why their fathers or mothers no longer came home at night, joined them at the dinner table, read them a bedtime story, helped them with their schoolwork. Faith could not provide answers to their children's demanding questions. One mother expressed exasperation at her child's queries:

> [My son] lays on the floor and he says "Mommy, I play dead so I can be with my Daddy."
>
> He's actually a lot more angry than my older son, and he's angry at God. "Why did God take my Daddy?" You know, "Why did he take him?" And this is an everyday occurrence, which I didn't think was going to happen with him. I thought—I definitely thought my older one, but not with him.
>
> And he does this every day, eight or ten times a day, "Why doesn't my Daddy come home? Why did God take him?"

By the end of the 9/11 program, I had developed a new awareness concerning the role of religion and faith in confronting tragedy, especially unanticipated death and injury. Some families' belief in God and trust in an afterlife helped them cope with their loss. Others were more skeptical but nevertheless buttressed their day-today life with the memory and spirit of the lost loved one. These families were not devout—9/11 had shaken their faith—but at the same time they were not ready to disavow God. Their reliance on religion was shaken, but faith was still present in their lives, almost as a form of hope in explaining the unexplainable. How else could they account for the tragedy, except through acceptance of some omnipresent, all-powerful deity?

Still others renounced religion entirely. Either there was no God or God had betrayed them, freeing them from all religious obligation. In any event, they could no longer rely on faith to get them through the day.

During one hearing, a wife and mother who lost her husband on 9/11 testified that her grieving son—unable to cope with the death of his father—committed suicide a few months later. September 11 had taken the lives of both her husband and her son. And what about her faith? Her lawyer at the hearing explained the dilemma:

> [This spouse and mother] is a steady church attender and has, I hope, an unshakable faith in God. But she called me after the death of her son and she said, "How am I supposed to be able to accept?" She alluded to the biblical Job, God testing one with one onslaught after another. I think she has been tested almost beyond endurance.

The "biblical Job"—the tale from the Hebrew Scriptures of the pious patriarch who endures undeserved suffering only to find his faith, in the end, strengthened by the ordeal—may provide the best lens through which to view the role of religion and faith in light of 9/11. Some survivors met the test and preserved, or even refortified, their faith. Others reached a breaking point. It was all a matter of individual conscience and outlook.

Inevitably, there were times during the hearings when sheer frustration overwhelmed every other emotion. The entire 9/11 tragedy provided fertile ground for immense frustration among the families—the fact that so many people said perfunctory good-byes to loved ones on that fateful sunny morning, never to see them again, only to confront complex, detailed application forms that seemingly placed cold dollar values on human beings lost forever. Many reeled in the face of the *unfairness* of life and the serendipitous nature of death.

Grief would gradually dissipate over time and anger would be assuaged; but not frustration. It would remain a formidable obstacle to the ultimate success of the fund.

Families whose lives were ripped asunder on 9/11 could never be disabused of the notion that they were the victims of a cruel trick selected at random by God, nature, or fate to suffer. "Why me?" they would ask. "My wife was such a good person; why did so many good people have to die?" Everybody associated with the fund knew that these questions had no answers. We could not comfort them. We were impotent in the face of their frustration.

The individual hearings brought this pervasive sense of frustration and helplessness to center stage. Claimant after claimant referred to the disconnect between a life lost and the inadequacy of mere compensation:

> Whatever award we receive will obviously never come close to the worth of our son. To be perfectly honest, this whole matter of victims' compensation is ghoulish and repulsive. We are in a no-win situation. Whatever we receive is not enough. The only way we win is if you had some magical power to bring [him] back.

This fact—that no amount of money could ever adequately reflect the value of a lost loved one—cast a shadow over the fund and became a serious impediment to our ultimate success.

I understood the families' reservations. How could a stranger, however well intentioned, put a monetary value on the life of a person he had never met? What did I know about the intrinsic moral worth of a wife or daughter? One wife spoke for many when she expressed her dissatisfaction with the Fund's entire rationale:

> First off, I just want to express my dissatisfaction with the victim compensation formula.
>
> I understand the process and why the fund was set up, but the formula that seems to have been used seems to eliminate the human factor.

The formula is based on statistics. [My husband] was not a statistic. He was a living, breathing, awesome person, who put his heart and soul into everything he did. And [my husband] spent his whole life helping others.... No amount of money can ever replace the life of my husband or ease the pain within our hearts.

The absence of a "human factor" in the process of calculating dollars and cents was not the only source of family frustration when it came to the fund. The complexity of the application process, and the fact that each claimant would likely receive a different amount of compensation, heightened anxiety. Many perceived the formulas as unfair because they valued one life more than another. Far from alleviating the unfairness of 9/11, they felt that the fund added to its arbitrariness:

The humane and simple thing to do would have been to just award each family X amount of dollars, the same for each person.... because, you know, the process would have been simpler ... You know, we were not in a mind set to be dealing with all of these things at that time, and we're still not, really.... it's been draining, physically, emotionally, and it's really been hard.

We've come to the point now where my son's life has been measured and reduced to tables, percentages and numbers, and the fact that he was single further reduces those numbers, and it seems to reduce the compensation or the award that I'm going to get simply because I'm a parent.... And the fact that, you know, that they consider his life a little bit—the numbers are less, let me put it that way, there's no other way I can put it, is hurtful. That's one of the most hurtful things I found in this process, aside from the fact that we had to collect all the data and jump through all the hoops and, you know, fill out all the forms. That was a long and draining process.

Other families expressed similar hurt when applying to the fund:

> I never dreamed that over a year this was going to turn into a nightmare. I was under the impression that the government was trying to help us and be fair...I'm totally frustrated and all of this just adds to the stress of all that has happened...For me, I wish I [had] never done it.... to have to go into a room and find paperwork, to finish this thing, has almost made me sick.

Another source of frustration was the public nature of 9/11. It was hard to escape daily reminders of what had happened. September 11 would always be front and center; private grief would rest uneasy next to public pain. Survivors attempting to start a new life would be forever drawn back—headlines on the heroism of those lost, "feel-good" stories of surviving families making do, the charitable impulses of friends and neighbors. It was everywhere. As one frustrated mother complained:

> September 11th isn't over yet, okay. It's in my—my son has a new social studies book, and it's smack in their face again. He has to do current events, and it's in their faces again. It's like the scab gets ripped right off of their healing process.

Frustration was most conspicuous in cases involving physical injuries. Surviving victims appeared at the hearings to explain how difficult it was for them to make out lives after 9/11. Survivors—horribly burned, disfigured, and emotionally scarred—would visit my office and calmly describe how they managed to escape that day, but how their lives would never be the same. A heightened sense of frustration was also expressed by injured rescue workers who were unable to reach victims before the collapse of the World Trade Center towers. Firefighters, police officers, and Port Authority personnel all testified about the permanent emotional scars they suffered because of their inability to respond to cries of help on 9/11. They had been beaten back by smoke, flames, and the catastrophic nature of the attacks. Rescue of many victims, especially those trapped in the higher floors above airplane impact points, was simply impossible. They knew this and yet they blamed themselves. The human frustration in hearing voices begging for help and watching people leap to their deaths became an emotional breaking point for many claimants:

The only thing that disturbed all of us was the fact that, in actuality, there was nobody to save. There was nobody to save. What we had been trained to do every day—to mend bones, to patch up wounds and treat people—that was not to be that day.

And it's amazing to me to think how many EMTs have left the field since then because they couldn't handle what they remember of that day, and have gone on to other things.

But you know the worst part? The worst part was when we responded over the Verrazano Bridge and looked into the city, and we could hear on our radio all these men trapped in the various parts of the buildings, screaming for help or giving out their location, "We're here, we're there, we're here." And, you know, as time went on, the calls got less and less and less.

Finally, there was the sense of frustration frequently brought on by family squabbling. Under the pressure of determining how to allocate a large tax-free payment at a time of horrible trauma, decades-old family disagreements suddenly surfaced anew. The loss of a loved one somehow dissolved the glue that had held the family together. In such cases, money actually became irrelevant; the hearing became a forum for families to unleash invective at one another, to express frustration at a family once united and now in chaos:

And because of that day, our family was cut out of our brother's life... [the spouse and her family] were plotting and manipulating, all right, and pushing our family out of John's life. None of our relatives got in the funeral, my brother's funeral, okay . . . when we see all the media coverage in the newspaper, as far as the liaisons interacting with my brother's widow, and all of these people driving new vehicles, new trucks, going on vacation, living like they hit the lottery because our brother died—and that's exactly how it looks, okay. Squandering his estate. . . . We were just in effect pushed out of his whole life, okay, by the Fire Department, by these liaisons, and by my brother's wife, okay . . . and it's all because she's so afraid somebody's going to get money . . . what a disappointment.

It occasionally got ugly—and complicated. Competing lawyers would appear at the same hearing, as many as seven or eight, each asserting a priority claim for the money:

> The claimant requested that the collateral offsets be offset against the entire award and the remainder be divided equally between her and her three biological children . . .
> The claimant's children, counsel for the claimant's children . . . assert that they are entitled to share equally in the award based on the doctrine of equitable adoption . . .
> [The victim's] three biological children . . . request greater than 50 percent of the award . . .

> The ex-wife...claims a share of the award....
>
> [The victim's] parents submitted the first claim
> filed on behalf of [the victim], which is now being
> treated as a Statement of Interest. They seek part of
> the award.

On a few occasions parents were at odds with children, and the children fought with one another. Parents and stepchildren bickered the most. It was as if all the pent-up petty squabbles among family members that had simmered quietly while the victim was alive now came to a boil. Money—large amounts of it—now triggered family civil war.

I gradually came to realize that frustration and helplessness, unlike anger and grief, often defy any attempt to help, that the amorphousness of frustration and its multiple causes undercut any quick-fix solutions. In the 9/11 hearings, we could focus on specific causes of anger and the concrete nature of grief; but frustration proved a more intractable problem. When a claimant appeared before me purely to bemoan the fact that he or she had been dealt a losing hand as a result of 9/11, my options were limited. The best response focused on the contrasting good that remained despite the personal tragedies arising out of 9/11—the children who still blessed the home of the surviving spouse, other siblings providing comfort and support, and so on.

Fiancées were my toughest challenge. It was very trying for them to reflect on a life's partnership that would never be. Compounding the problem were the victims' biological parents who, immediately after 9/11, often rejected the very idea of the anticipated marriage. Women who days earlier were about to be welcomed into the family as daughters were now disowned by their onetime future in-laws; they would come to me in tears and bemoan their fate, telling me: "Mr. Feinberg, I was going to be married a few weeks after 9/11. The church had been selected and the invitations mailed. My future mother-in-law even hosted a shower on my behalf. Yet the day after 9/11, she would not even accept a phone call from me to share our grief."

The victim's parents responded: "The marriage was never going to take place. Our son was having second thoughts. She is not entitled to a dime."

I became convinced that disputes between fiancées and the victims' parents were not about greed but frustration: the fiancée cruelly and arbitrarily denied a life with her chosen partner, parents suddenly forced to confront their autumn years without a son or anticipated grandchildren. A future so promising had suddenly become a giant black hole. The cataclysmic suddenness of it all overwhelmed fiancées and parents alike, washing away yesterday's hopes and dreams. And so the parents tried to deny any living symbol of a future that would never be. They reacted with callousness and a strange insensitivity that was totally out of character. It was the only way they could cope. They had to rewrite history in order to change the last chapter.

In meeting with the fiancées, any conventional clichés—"You're young," "You have your whole life ahead of you"—rang hollow. There was little I could say that would comfort these individuals. Any share of the award that I could secure for them by using my mediation skills to negotiate with the victim's biological parents was accepted with appreciation and thanks. But the compensation was secondary. The lives of fiancées had been shattered.

In the end, I emphasized the value of memory in providing a permanent link to a happier past. Memory—once again—became the most valuable anodyne in my small chest of pain relievers.

need 犬

CHAPTER SIX

Solomon's Choices

IN THE END—after all the writing and revising of regulations, the scrutinizing of applications, the seemingly
endless rounds of town hall forums, informal meetings,
and individual family hearings—it fell to me to make the
agonizing choices that only the special master could
make.

In establishing the 9/11 fund, Congress had mandated
that eligible families and victims should receive different
levels of compensation depending on the financial hard-
ship visited upon the survivors. In so doing, Congress virtually guaranteed a heated economic and philosophic
debate revolving around the meaning and scope of
"need." Did the stockbroker's family "need" more compensation than the waiter's or the busboy's? Did the
banker's widow "need" more than the firefighter's spouse
or the family of the sergeant who died at the Pentagon?

The statute made me responsible for tailoring individual awards to meet the needs of each family. But I also knew that my tenure as special master would be short-lived if I paid tax-free awards in the double-digit millions. I refused to use the fund to subsidize extravagant lifestyles, but I recognized the dilemma: How much is enough?

Many families felt that the fund was obligated to help them preserve their pre–9/11 lifestyles. Since Congress had raised formidable obstacles to lawsuits, they believed they should receive the equivalent of a successful trip to the courthouse. They were *entitled* to public compensation that would keep two cars in the family garage, the kids in private school, and the Long Island summer home safe and secure:

> So we went to an architectural firm and came up with the plans that basically was our self-contained oasis. It has a home theater and an indoor pool, and it has the apartment for his parents...
>
> My kids have been in private pre-school since they were little, and now they're in—you know, they're in a private grade school that is just a phenomenal place for them...It's a wonderful place, and it's very expensive. So you know how much that costs.

"extravagant lifestyle"

Appealing on behalf of surviving young children was a common tactic: "The kids would be devastated. I think it's horrible enough that they lose their mom, let alone, you know, [they] have to move out of their house and their bedroom," one claimant argued.

diff. values

Some foreign claimants focused on cultural differences in lifestyle as a justification for greater compensation. One brother claimed his sister was planning on supporting their Indian parents, and that her intention to do so should be factored into the compensation:

> In fact, [the victim] went so far as to tell her father several years ago that it was not her intention to ever marry because she intended to continue to provide for her parents for the rest of their lives. She wanted to be available to her parents in their old age.…
>
> In our culture, in our heritage, it's normally the oldest son, meaning me. Even though I'm younger than the three sisters, it would have been my responsibility to take care of my parents. Because [the victim] said you have your own family and she said she'll assume the responsibility. And everything she did proved to me that she did, she was going to do that and it gave me a sense of assurance that she will do that.

take care of parents

Others defined "need" differently. It was not restoration of a former lifestyle that they sought, but rather recognition that their loved one had been cruelly wrenched from their lives without warning and without the opportunity to plan for future financial security. This entitled them to heftier compensation to fill a conspicuous void. Compensation in such cases was not tied to existing financial circumstances but rather to the replace-

loss of loved one financial security

ment value of a family anchor—someone who would no longer preside at the family dinner table, help the boys learn how to play baseball, and teach the girls how to read.

This inevitably led to hearings that focused on the strength, love, and wisdom of the victim.

These claimants demanded more money because of the victim's intrinsic moral worth. Since the husband and father was the perfect family man, since the wife and mother had sacrificed so much for the family, since the brother or sister was the glue that kept the family together, more was lost and therefore more was needed to compensate for the loss.

Unfortunately many 9/11 families came to believe that the fund was attempting to place a dollar value on the life of the victim. It took years to disabuse families of this notion. The fund was *not* valuing the moral worth of those murdered on 9/11. I reaffirmed this whenever I met publicly with families at community meetings or privately with a particular claimant. Instead, I emphasized the requirement of need, which was linked directly to financial circumstances.

But sometimes arguments about need crossed the border into the ridiculous. One spouse who had lost his wife at the World Trade Center hinted that his award should be enough to pay for services that can't be legally purchased: "I don't want to sound gross, but there is something else that I pay for, or can pay for. You can figure that out . . . there are other services that could be replaced, but we're not going to go into that either." With a sense of disbelief, I gradually understood that he was asking the fund to help him pay for the services of prostitutes.

I rejected his request.

Most of the requests for larger awards were not driven by greed. For almost twenty years I had resolved complex disputes and allocated hundreds of millions of dollars to eligible claimants. My experience had taught me to recognize when clients and their lawyers were demanding more than the merits of the dispute warranted. I never came to believe that the 9/11 families consciously manufactured specious arguments and inflated claims in order to maximize their awards. They simply played by the rules.

The problem was with the statute, which required inquiry into the murky and unpredictable world of economic loss. "Need" was the statutory constant. So the families tailored their arguments to emphasize need. I had no problem with this. Given the rules by which the fund operated, the families' reaction was virtually preordained.

Was it greedy of the 9/11 families to want to maximize the awards they received? No. By ordering the special master to determine varying payout amounts for each claimant, the law created a scale of victimhood, measured in dollars. Under the circumstances, I can't blame the families for feeling that they "deserved" at least as much money as other claimants. After all, wasn't their suffering unique? Wasn't their loss unfathomable?

social engineering

Wasn't the value of their missing loved one incalculable?
To accept a lesser payment would be insulting to the
memory of the departed. The families *had* to ask for
more.

KF's original goal *

As the award decisions fell into place, one by one, I
stuck to my original goals of minimizing the number of
very large and very small payments while narrowing the
overall gap between the wealthy and those of modest
means. Social engineering, yes—but designed to carry out
what I believe Congress intended and what the American
people wanted. My strategy was based on both practical
and political considerations. As Senator Kennedy had
warned me, if 15 percent of the families got 85 percent of
the grants—tax free—I would have been pilloried. So I
didn't let that happen.

Week by week, I kept track of the payout statistics as
they evolved. Over time, the average award gradually
increased—not because my standards shifted but because,
as the deadline for participation in the fund drew near,
more of the high-end families opted to forgo the right to
sue in favor of our guaranteed awards. According to the
final statistics, the average award for a death claim was
just over $2 million (see Appendix). More importantly,
the median award (the "middle" award, with exactly half
the claimants receiving more and half receiving less) was
just shy of $1.7 million. Note the relatively narrow gap
between the two statistics. This demonstrates that I succeeded in keeping the size of the awards under control. If
extremely large payments to wealthy families had been

average & mean close

made, they would have skewed the average such that the gap between average and median would have been much higher. I avoided this.

Many economically privileged families sharply criticized me for my policy choice. A few even initiated a lawsuit in an attempt to curtail my personal discretion. Their arguments were heard and rejected by both the Federal District Court, and the Second Circuit Court of Appeals in New York. As the judges recognized, Congress wanted me to use my discretion as a safety valve to prevent the very outcome the few wealthiest families sought—tax-free payouts in the double-digit millions to a select group of claimants.

One or two of the press accounts of my work referred to my "Robin Hood" approach. I don't think the description fits. The legendary bandit was famous for "taking from the rich to give to the poor." But I didn't do that at all. The 9/11 fund had no overall appropriation to be parceled out, so the amount given to one person couldn't possibly affect the amount someone else would receive. I didn't take anything away from the rich; all I did was make certain that rich and poor alike received their fair share according to the statute.

As the filing deadline of December 22, 2003, drew near, many observers of the fund program, including members of my staff, grew anxious. As of the start of September, fewer than 2,400 eligible families and injured victims had applied—fewer than one-third of the estimated total. The fund's success remained in doubt. Why weren't more family members filing with the fund? Why would a spouse, mother, father, or child choose not to complete an application form that would bring them a tax-free $2 million? Where were the physical injury victims? Why weren't they applying? What could we do to convince them to act in time?

One of our outreach tools was the web page on the Justice Department site devoted to the 9/11 fund. Here we posted information about awards recently issued, limited by the requirement that no names or addresses of claimants be disclosed in order to preserve the confidentiality of the process.

(We took our obligation to maintain confidentiality very seriously. I knew from family accounts that all the major New York newspapers—the *Times*, the *Post,* and the *Daily News*—assigned reporters to track down specific 9/11 claimants and link them to particular payment amounts, in hopes of writing intriguing "human interest" stories about these tragic victims and the large sums they received. I could see the journalistic logic—such stories would combine a touching tale of tragic loss with the excitement of a "Local Woman Wins Lottery Jackpot" story. But to this day the papers have failed to unearth the information they sought—that's how tightly we protected the families' privacy.)

Our website was designed to promote transparency

without violating the rule of confidentiality. Thus a potential fund participant could read on the site about the range of payments that we'd made that week, along with some basic information about the recipient—"A wage earner earning X, with a wife and two kids, received an award of Y." We wanted to let the public see what we were doing—it was taxpayer money after all—without breaching confidentiality.

The transparency helped matters. So did word of mouth among those who received payments. Any time an award was sent to a family living in the same neighborhood with other 9/11 victims, it created a ripple effect of applications. Once the word went out that Mrs. J. down the block had really received $2 million tax free, with no strings attached, this was enough to convince her friends Mrs. M and Mr. N that the fund was a legitimate program worthy of participation. As the end of 2003 loomed, the flow of applications dramatically increased.

Still, there were unaccountable stragglers. At staff meetings we would share stories of disbelief: the mother who refused to leave her bed to fill out the forms pertaining to her dead son; the spouse seated at the kitchen table with a glassy stare unable to focus on me as I explained the benefits of the fund. Each story was more heart-wrenching than the next.

Some parents couldn't acknowledge the death of their child, as if doing so would ratify the horror of 9/11. One father struggled with denial:

I don't believe in this, that my son died on September
11th. This is all kind of baloney. My son is working
in some other state. He's alive and he is not—he's not
dead.... This is what I feel in my heart. And about a
week ago I felt he was kind of changing his shape or
whatever, his appearance.

I learned to deal with my frustration over what I saw
as irresponsible family behavior. I convinced myself that,
in the end, reason would prevail and families overwhelmed with grief would file with the fund. But my frustration mounted as more and more families expressed a
reluctance or an inability to file early, citing grief, anger,
confusion, or occasionally a "wait-and-see" attitude.
Some continued to question the legitimacy and bona fides
of the fund itself. "Are you really giving me $2 million
tax free? I don't believe it," they would say. To families
victimized by a cruel, irrational universe, such generosity
only heightened their general skepticism, cynicism, confusion, and suspicion.

Until the final days of the program, its success—measured by family participation—remained in doubt. Many
9/11 families, paralyzed by grief and despair, remained
on the fence, unable to decide whether or not to apply to
the fund. Only at the end, as the fund's statutory deadline
approached, did the families and victims finally resign
themselves to practical realities. They could no longer
defer decisions until a sunnier tomorrow. Lobbied by relatives and friends, their attorneys, my staff, and me, they

slowly came to recognize how compensation could help them rebuild their fractured lives.

A couple of well-meaning members of Congress raised the possibility of extending the application deadline. Why not give the fund a little extra time to entice the stragglers? Senator Kennedy suggested the idea.

"Don't you dare," I responded. I knew from my past experience as a mediator that deadline pressure is a *good* thing—indeed, an essential device to force action. Extending the deadline would only encourage further procrastination. The idea was dropped.

In the last few days, reality set in and applications flooded in during November and December. Over 40 percent of all eligible claimants filed their claims during the sixty days prior to the deadline, including two-thirds of those injured on 9/11. By midnight on December 22, 2003, 97 percent of eligible families had decided to opt into the fund; thousands of the injured also signed up. Vindicated by the sheer number of claims, the 9/11 fund was a major success.

Still, when the statutory deadline expired and the dust settled, an estimated seven families of deceased victims had not availed themselves of either option. Paralyzed by grief, clinically depressed, they sat on the sidelines and avoided the hard decisions that closed the final chapter of a life. In meeting personally with some of these seven families, I glimpsed the devastating impact of depression and sorrow on their lives. But I was an outsider looking in. I could never stand in their shoes or understand the depth of a grief that left them unable to function. These seven families were inconsolable. They could not act.

I met with mothers who had lost sons and begged them to complete the necessary application forms: "Mrs. Jones, I will help you," I said. "Just sign the form and my staff will fill out the rest of the application. Don't compound the tragedy of 9/11 by missing the statutory deadline. You will be surrendering the right to receive $2 million. Take the money. Establish a foundation in your son's name. Don't let the terrorists win."

Mrs. Jones stared at me blankly. In a flat, robotic tone she responded, "Go away, Mr. Feinberg. Thank you for coming but no amount of money can replace him. Leave the application on the kitchen table. I'll look at it later." I never heard from her and the application was never filed.

Why would a family forgo the opportunity to receive millions? At the beginning, I was stunned by some people's inability to function in the wake of the tragedy. But, over time, I came to understand. These people were in such pain that they were unable to act. I sought out relatives, friends, coworkers, clergy to intercede. With their help, I convinced most of the mourners to file a claim. But in those estimated seven cases, I failed. And since Congress never extended the filing deadline for these few families, they are forever locked out of the program.

The plight of these unhappy few was my single biggest disappointment in administering the fund.

CHAPTER SEVEN

Looking Back

THE SEPTEMBER 11th Victim Compensation Fund of 2001 was a stunning success. The vast majority of interested parties—our elected officials, the public, and the 9/11 families—eventually came onboard. The controversy that initially characterized the program gradually yielded to a type of studied calm as the program took shape, then to a grudging acceptance, and finally to admiration.

I was helped in my efforts by overwhelming public support. The American people not only endorsed the program but embraced it. The few critics who spoke out against the fund were overwhelmed by public enthusiasm for it. The editorial pages of the *New York Times, Washington Post, Chicago Tribune,* and other major newspapers offered support for my efforts. Television and radio programs first commiserated with my difficult task, then urged me on to success by highlighting the generosity and

criteria of success

compassion of the American people. I got plenty of encouragement from ordinary citizens too. Strangers would stop me at airports, introduce themselves, and then comment: "I don't envy your job. I just want to thank you for taking on such a thankless task. Keep up the good work."

Members of the House and Senate wisely stayed far away from the program, rarely offering public comments about the fund while privately congratulating me and prodding me onwards. If there was ever a bipartisan groundswell of political support for a federal program, this was it. Everybody wanted the fund to work. And it did.

The fund graduated with highest honors. Indeed, I believe it can fairly be considered the valedictorian of all compensation programs, public or private. Statistics tell part of the story. Ninety-seven percent of eligible families who suffered a loss on 9/11—2,880 individuals filing claims on behalf of deceased victims—entered the program. They received almost $6 billion in tax-free compensation. In addition, over 4,400 physical injury victims decided that the fund offered a better route than a trip to the courthouse; of these, 2,682 received over $1 billion in compensation.

① participation rate

The fund validated the congressional decision to divert potential tort claims away from a beleaguered airline industry. Fewer than ninety people ultimately opted to sue the airlines and other entities (the World Trade Center, the airports, Boeing, the airport security compa-

② <90 lawsuits against airlines, others

nies) rather than enter the fund. I wish them good fortune, but I remain convinced that they made a mistake in choosing not to join the fund. As a lawyer, I consider their chance of winning their lawsuits quite slim. And as for their other objective—to use the lawsuits as leverage to force disclosures about our nation's preparedness for the 9/11 attack—I explained to them that they would have greater success pursuing that goal through the 9/11 Commission and the Senate and House Intelligence Committees.

The final numbers also make clear that I successfully exercised my discretion as special master to assure that tax-free dollars would not be skewed in the direction of high income families. Over 43 percent of all families filing a death claim with the fund had income levels under $100,000; less than 7 percent claimed income over $1 million. I succeeded in "bringing down the top and bringing up the bottom," in order to narrow the gap between rich and poor.

Finally, the fund operated very efficiently. Although the complexity of the claim assessment program required a staff of nearly 450 employees (at the program's height), in the end administrative costs amounted to just 1.2 percent of the total funds disbursed. This is a ratio that surpasses virtually any charitable or nonprofit organization.

How do I account for the fund's success? The *Final Report,* which I delivered to President Bush on June 15, 2004, summarized the reasons why families eventually embraced the program:

Why was it successful

To the extent that participation is a measure of success, the Fund was extraordinarily successful. What factors contributed to this success? In our view, there are five major factors that resulted in this overwhelming acceptance of the Fund as a means of compensation.

(1) *poor BATNA*

First, the alternative of litigation presented both

(2) *transparency*

uncertainty and delay. Second, the Fund took extraordinary steps to assure that families could obtain detailed information about their likely recovery from the Fund. Third, the Fund took a proactive

(3) *proactive & personal approach*

approach—personally contacting each claimant, ensuring that claimants were able to obtain and present the best information in support of the claim; assisting claimants in obtaining helpful information; explaining to claimants information that would assist the Fund in maximizing the computation of economic loss and resolving uncertainties in favor of the

(4) *gave claimants their "day in court" to be heard*

claimant. Fourth, the Fund offered in-person informal meetings along with hearings so that claimants could "have their day in court" and explain the magnitude of their loss and their views about the way in which the Fund should treat their particular situation. Fifth, the Fund offered certainty without significant delay, allowing families the option of a type of

(5)

"closure."

Add to these policy decisions the more personal reasons for the fund's success. I was given a unique assignment by the attorney general. I recognized the historic magnitude of the task. If I failed, if the program proved a disaster, I would forever be remembered as an unimaginative government functionary who foolishly took on an impossible burden and allowed his ambition to cloud his judgment. To me, failure was not an option. Personal doggedness and determination, therefore, characterized my everyday conduct throughout the three years that I worked for the fund.

I also benefited, frankly, from low public expectations concerning the program, and even lower expectations among the 9/11 families. Paradoxically, skepticism about the fund worked to my advantage. Every small step I took to improve the image and administration of the program helped earn it public acceptance and grudging family support. The fund's credibility evolved over time, as an increasing number of critics turned full circle and offered their support. Clouds of doubt and suspicion gave way to an atmosphere of hope and encouragement.

Charles Wolf, who lost his wife on one of the doomed airliners on 9/11, personally symbolized the gradual shift in attitude. During the early months of the program, he operated as a kind of self-appointed gadfly, constantly monitoring and challenging my decisions in administering the fund. He criticized our policies regarding noneconomic loss calculations, collateral offsets, and the refusal to recognize psychological injuries alongside physical ones, among other issues. He turned up at one town hall meeting after another, often greeting me with a handshake and a remark like, "Hello, Ken—I'm here to criticize the fund once again." He even launched a website, titled "Fix the Fund," which he used to air his grievances.

I maintained open communication with Charles Wolf, not changing my policies when I thought they were right but allowing him his say alongside the other family members. Gradually Wolf began to appreciate the fund and the sincerity of our efforts. Some six months prior to the filing deadline, he changed the name of his website from "Fix the Fund" to "The Fund Is Fixed." Even more gratifying, he began standing up at family meetings to say, "I've come around to being a supporter of Ken Feinberg's leadership. If you haven't sent in your application, you ought to do it. The fund deserves our participation."

My relationship with other families also improved over time. Critics congratulated me for "changing my attitude," "becoming less arrogant," and "finally being sensitive to family needs." I hope that I did become more effective in communicating on behalf of the fund. But I also believe that the 9/11 families changed, slowly coming to recognize the value of the fund and my determination to help them. The initial skepticism and mistrust they directed at me as the visible symbol of the government gradually yielded to mutual understanding and respect. Even though I was not one of them—I could *never* be one of them—at least I became a good listener, like an understanding friend who arrives on the scene of a family tragedy ready to help.

I also was fortunate to enjoy the complete support of the attorney general, the Department of Justice, and the White House. Even in the fund's darkest days, Attorney General John Ashcroft went out of his way to offer personal advice and encouragement. I developed a genuine fondness and respect for him. He offered me wise counsel and made sound substantive suggestions. I will always be in his debt.

Any explanation of the fund's success must also acknowledge the extraordinary generosity of the American people: over $7 billion in tax-free compensation. The Congress took the extraordinary step of funding the program out of general revenues. No fixed congressional appropriation accompanied the new law. Instead, the statute simply authorized me to spend whatever was necessary to secure fund objectives.

As for me, I am often asked about the personal impact the fund had on me over the past three years. In addition to family and friends expressing concern about the physical and mental strain of my work, strangers approach me and ask in a hesitant tone recognizing the demarcation line that separates the private from the public: "How did it affect you? How have you changed? Will you ever be the same?"

I give the standard answers to strangers: "We all change; we wouldn't be human if we failed to respond to life's highs and lows." But this is, of course, a diversionary tactic, an easy way out, a halfhearted attempt to deflect the hard questions and avoid introspection. After thirty-two months of working on the fund, I find such questions hard to address. Even today.

At first, I rationalized that, as a professional, I might find these questions a threat to my task of maintaining objectivity and avoiding self-doubt and second-guessing. Like the doctor who steels himself from becoming too emotionally involved with his patients, I couldn't afford to become the victim of my own doubts about the program and its impact. I tried to build an emotional wall to protect me from too much self-analysis.

The program has now been completed successfully, yet I still run away from such questions. My reasons are varied and complex, but ultimately they come down to the fact that such inquiries force me to consider, in a calm and detached manner, the impact of 9/11 on me as an individual. I don't relish that. Like most Americans, I'd prefer to escape from 9/11. I've sat with too many sobbing parents and confused children, cut loose in life without a father or mother. It is too painful for me.

But, of course, I can't look into the mirror each morning and totally evade self-analysis. The program changed my life in large and small ways.

On the most obvious level, my career path has changed dramatically. After managing the 9/11 fund, I am a bit unfulfilled mediating another dispute between two Fortune 500 companies. So I've shifted the focus of my professional life, starting with a radical downsizing of my law firm. Today, I devote much of my energy to educating the next generation of lawyers. I teach mass torts at the University of Pennsylvania, Columbia, Georgetown, and Virginia. I continue to mediate disputes that I find particularly interesting and meaningful—for example, a major case involving accusations of sexual abuse in an archdiocese of the Roman Catholic Church or a racial discrimination class action suit brought by Hispanic police officers in New York City. I pick and choose cases in a desire to do some good for both the litigants and the broader society in which I live.

On a personal level, I've undoubtedly become much more fatalistic about life and death. Whoever is pulling the strings, whatever cosmic force is making the call, it's clear to me that life and death can turn on the most innocuous events—requesting a second cup of coffee at a local diner, a ten-minute delay that miraculously prevents you from being trapped in your office in the World Trade Center; accompanying your child to school one day, which prevents you from being at your desk in the Pentagon when the plane hits; surviving the destruction at the World Trade Center by sheer luck, while your fellow rescue workers, standing next to you, become part of the fatality count. The random nature of who lives and who dies was a common thread throughout the life of the 9/11 fund.

I now feel it's a mistake to plan too far ahead, to assume that life will conform to my expectations. Life is fickle and unpredictable. I've become profoundly skeptical of those master of the universe types who map out the future oblivious to the possibility, even the likelihood, of misfortune—the businessman who accepts a new job convinced that he will be promoted twice in five years and be made a senior executive; the law student who tells me that she will join a law firm and rise to partner; the young mother who informs me that she plans to have three more children. I listen and nod and smile, and I wonder whether any of this will come to pass. Where is it written that life will be so accommodating?

Compassion has also become more important to me. I try hard to be more caring in my day-to-day living. The 9/11 families have had a profound impact on how I approach relationships with family, friends, and others. I think I've become a better listener. I no longer offer advice gratuitously without thinking of consequences. I try to give more careful answers. I try harder to understand the viewpoints of others. And I'm more accepting of human flaws and foibles.

I am often asked whether, in retrospect, I regret accepting the job of special master. I knew the job was going to be hard and I would do it again if unfortunate circumstances required. I also believe that my pro bono service set an example for the nation. I have no doubt that millions of Americans would have done what I did, would have willingly served as special master without pay. Instead, they contributed in other ways, pouring private donations into charities in unprecedented amounts. Such donations—and the 9/11 fund—are lasting testaments to the inherent goodness and compassion of the American people.

In recent months, I've heard from a few of the 9/11 families, their lawyers and friends, writing to thank me for my work. One commented, "The fund cannot bring back those who died, but it can keep alive the victims' dreams for their families." That was my primary goal, and the fund accomplished it to a degree most of us never expected. I was particularly moved by the comments of a lawyer, Larry Stewart, representing a family at one of the hearings. Stewart was a key figure in getting Congress to create the fund, and his words will always resonate with me:

I also would like to state something on the record. And that is that these families all owe a tremendous debt to you. What you have done is beyond words in running this program. I know that there were some rocky times at the beginning, but I think it is a testament to what you have achieved that almost 100 percent have filed claims.

My own personal experience has been, in talking to many of these families, that I do not know of a single family that has come away from this process who has not felt that they were fairly treated, with dignity and respect and compassion, with sympathy. And all of them have said, in one way or another, that as difficult as it was, they felt essentially good about it at the end, and that the awards that they received were fair under the circumstances.

I am frequently asked whether the 9/11 families will stay in contact with me, whether there will be reunions to reinforce the personal relationships I developed with the families over the past few years. Surely, it is suggested, I should do all I can to preserve these relationships and provide additional comfort to those trying desperately to piece their lives back together. Wouldn't periodic meetings be helpful?

I don't think so. The fund filled a void following 9/11. It provided generous compensation to families in grief, alleviating major concerns—financial and psychological—that would have caused additional torment at a time of personal vulnerability and uncertainty. But now the page has turned. Today the 9/11 families confront the future with varying degrees of optimism, security, and hope. Some spouses have already remarried; others are raising their children with increasing confidence as single parents. Children who were teenagers on 9/11 are now in college, and infants with no firsthand memories of a lost parent are now in school, adjusting to a world where their questions about a parent they never knew are as much a part of history as an expression of personal curiosity.

Annual reunions would serve no beneficial purpose. The closure achieved by 9/11 families in entering the fund should remain secure. Future generations can review the record and discuss why the fund was created and debate its merits. But the families themselves should remember the fund as a unique response by the American people that helped the families get on with their lives. Constant reminders would not be warranted. In fact, the degree to which the 9/11 families have begun to move on into the next chapter of their lives is perhaps the most important measurement—more meaningful than mere statistics—of the success of the fund.

CHAPTER EIGHT

Looking Ahead: Lessons for the Future

AMERICANS HOPE and pray that another tragedy like 9/11 will never occur. But it would be unrealistic and irresponsible not to anticipate such an attack. The Department of Homeland Security, the attorney general, the director of the FBI, and the president have all warned that subsequent acts of foreign terrorism here at home are not only possible but likely. We are asked to be ever vigilant, ready to repel any would-be terrorist threat.

In the wake of another terrorist attack, there will undoubtedly be calls for a new compensation program. Now that a no-fault public compensation fund has been tested and found to be a success, there is likely to be support for another fund designed to help Americans devastated by terrorism. It is important, therefore, to ask, What lessons have we learned from the 9/11 fund experience? Are compensation funds a good idea? How should they be structured and administered? Who should be eligible for these payments? How much money should they get?

My short answer to these crucial questions is simple: I think it would be a mistake for Congress or the public to take the 9/11 fund as a precedent for similar programs. Despite its success, I would not use the fund as a model in the event of future attacks.

I have several reasons for taking this stance. The first harkens back to the question of eligibility discussed earlier in this book—the issue of why the 9/11 victims were given special treatment as compared with the victims of the Oklahoma City bombing, the first World Trade Center attack, the USS Cole, and other tragedies.

If the 9/11 fund is regarded as a model, why shouldn't all of life's misfortunes be subject to public compensation? Why not provide all victims of terrorism, as well as those who die in floods, earthquakes, or hit-and-run accidents, similar compensation? They too are innocent victims of the unforeseen. And what about the true hero who dies in an effort to save others? Isn't public compensation justified in such a case? Surely society wants to encourage such selfless acts of heroism. Compensation would send a community signal that heroic acts of rescue should be rewarded.

I have thought about these questions for hours, usually in the middle of a sleepless night anticipating a meeting with a widow from Oklahoma City or a parent who lost a child in a tenement fire or a Mississippi flood. I have concluded that public compensation would not work in any of these cases. Why not?

why not

First, there's the notion, deeply ingrained in our national character, that in a free society people make choices and live—and die—by them. Where to live, work, and go to school. What risks to take. What dangers to avoid. Government does not act as an insurer of last resort to compensate those who die as a result of their own choices or life's misfortunes. Free choice, self-reliance, "the road not taken"—these concepts are so embedded in our culture that a public compensation program designed to protect us against unforeseen misfortune is an alien notion, inconsistent with liberty.

The second reason is another principle of American life—that government should be limited rather than becoming involved every time a citizen suffers a personal blow. Yes, the government may come to the rescue by providing basic benefits such as low-cost loans to rebuild homes and emergency assistance after a hurricane or earthquake. But the government shouldn't pay out millions in personal compensation for death or injury as an entitlement owed to each citizen. That is unsound public policy, and it runs counter to the American tradition of self-reliance.

There is also a practical concern. Individual responsibility is undercut when citizens believe that the government will bail them out if they act unreasonably and thereby cause or suffer harm. Why be careful if the government stands ready to compensate the victim whenever unforeseen tragedy occurs? The idea that you are responsible for your own bad actions and must suffer their consequences lies at the heart of our civil justice system. If lawsuits are replaced with a generous no-fault public, tax-free compensation program, why worry about causing injury to others? A statutory no-fault program extended to a wide range of injuries would undermine personal responsibility.

This is why the 9/11 fund isn't a precedent for reform of the tort system, a goal sought by many in Congress and in the Bush administration (as well as many of the business executives who seek my comments after hearing me speak about my experiences). I'm convinced that the civil justice system is an important force for promoting safe standards of conduct and individual responsibility. It protects citizens against the drunk driver, the reckless landlord who creates a fire hazard, and the negligent corporation that manufactures a harmful drug or chemical. Important consequences flow, therefore, from any comprehensive attempt to restrict the scope of the private litigation system. Occasionally it is necessary to do so; in the context of 9/11, moving to protect the shaky airline industry could be justified on broad economic (and political) grounds. Expanding this exception and making it the rule across the board would be something else entirely.

Other practical considerations argue against an expansion of the 9/11 fund. American society has long relied on private insurance and other free market initiatives to act as a hedge against the unforeseen. Any attempt to replace our current system of private health, injury, and life insurance with a pervasive new compensation program similar to the 9/11 fund would profoundly change the way we respond to death, injury, and misfortune, creating unpredictable political controversies and economic dislocations. Recent attempts to develop a new, modified partnership between government and the private sector in such diverse areas as Medicare, Social Security, and terrorist property damage insurance, immediately fuel controversy.

For all these reasons, the 9/11 fund should remain limited to the unique circumstances that gave it birth. Attempts to replicate it in other contexts are neither necessary, practical, nor philosophically justifiable.

Surprisingly, the uniqueness of the 9/11 fund has been recognized by victims of other tragedies. I received some "Why not me?" demands from next of kin in Oklahoma City and elsewhere but not very many. This may be the most important point of all. The special circumstances of the 9/11 tragedy seem to be acknowledged by others who arguably had reason to demand similar financial treatment.

I was particularly intrigued by the muted Oklahoma response, which may be partly explained by the culture and history of Oklahoma and the American West. I believe there is a pioneer-style resignation among these families, a recognition that life is full of unavoidable risks and hazards. Overcome the obstacles and move forward; be resolute in your determination to make out a life; don't whine or seek excuses; don't expect excessive generosity, gifts or handouts. Instead, steel your resolve and remain independent. I recognized these characteristics of self-reliance in the refusal of Oklahoma City families and victims to criticize the fund.

The families who lost loved ones in the Kenya embassy bombings and in the attack on the USS *Cole* were also reluctant to criticize the 9/11 fund. Their loved ones had volunteered to stand in harm's way. Risk went with the territory. Very few sought compensation from the fund. They simply did not believe it appropriate to do so. Nor did the victims of other misfortunes—a hit-and-run accident, a drowning, a fire fatality—apply to the Fund. They sensed that the government was not some paternal guarantor. Most Americans, perhaps unconsciously, value individual independence, self-reliance, and personal integrity. Government may assist them in extreme circumstances, but it must not undercut these fundamental elements of the American character.

In the end, the American people recognized the unusual historic circumstances surrounding 9/11 and supported the creation of a unique victim compensation program for that tragedy. Very few American citizens would opt to expand the program to encompass all of life's uncertainties and tragedies. But what if we did suffer another terrorist attack on our soil akin to 9/11? Would Americans support another compensation program along the lines of the 9/11 fund? Would Congress enact it? Should it?

I don't believe that Congress should repeat the 9/11 fund precedent in creating a compensation formula that pegs awards to individual economic circumstances. This was, of course, the heart and soul of the 9/11 fund. But, I've become convinced that <u>the 9/11 fund formula was defective.</u> Instead, if Congress decides to provide compensation in the event of a new terrorist attack, <u>all eligible claimants should receive the same amount.</u>

There are numerous practical reasons for this.

<u>First,</u> any statutory compensation formula that recognizes and reinforces economic distinctions among claimants is guaranteed to <u>promote divisiveness</u> among the very families it seeks to help. This is an important lesson I learned from my meetings with victims' families. Despite my admonition—"Don't count other people's money"—families couldn't help but compare their awards with the amounts provided to their next-door neighbors. And so the relative value of awards became a dominant feature of the fund, pitting firefighters against accountants, army officers against bond traders, police officers against busboys.

Of course juries routinely weigh economic loss in determining the size of awards. But in the context of an organized compensation program, this analogy isn't compelling. The 9/11 families weren't in a courtroom setting where a jury would listen to each case individually and render distinct verdicts. Instead, the families were all roped into the same program. They bumped up against each other and compared notes. They dissected similarities and differences. The fund rules encouraged them to shop comparatively and inquire into relative worth.

In short, the statute creating the fund exacerbated the

raw wounds of 9/11 by creating an economic hierarchy tied to the victims' individual economic success. It had the opposite effect of that intended by Congress—at least at the beginning. Instead of healing wounds and uniting the families, it fueled resentment and paranoia among them. It also made my job harder, promoting the perception that I was denigrating the lives of victims who received smaller sums.

In addition, many families viewed the payments as "hush money." They felt the fund was trying to entice grieving families into the program—and away from the courtroom—by paying them off. In this view, the real goal of the fund was to prevent the families from pursuing embarrassing lawsuits that might reveal who in government was responsible for the 9/11 tragedy. It took years and a major outreach effort for me to overcome such attitudes. But the effort was slow and painful.

Then there are practical concerns. It's extremely time-consuming to calculate economic loss for thousands of claimants. Faced with the dizzying array of statistics and facts that make up a life, it's difficult to separate fact from fantasy, the real from the speculative. We had to take time with each claim, checking and rechecking it. As a result, to a certain extent we undercut the very purpose of the statute—to provide speedy compensation rather than protracted litigation in the courtroom.

Any future program to compensate victims of a foreign terrorist attack here at home would be better based on the principle of uniformity—the same amount paid to all eligible claimants. Individual wealth or the economic circumstances of surviving next of kin should play no role in the computation of awards. The family of the stockbroker and that of the dishwasher should receive the same check from the United States Treasury.

But would it?

This approach would minimize claimant divisiveness by avoiding the task of placing a "value" on the life of a lost loved one. It would also provide a streamlined process for the speedy payment of claims. The special master would no longer need a supporting army of accountants and statisticians. His sole job would be to determine eligibility.

As a model, I suggest following workers' compensation statutes, which provide uniform payments to workers injured on the job. The mechanic who mangles his hand working a lathe receives the same payments as the piano player suffering from carpal tunnel syndrome. The economic circumstances surrounding the two applicants—how much their homes are worth, how many dependents they have, the value of their savings and checking accounts—are irrelevant.

Nor should collateral sources of income be deducted from awards. If the stockbroker's widow receives the same amount as the police officer's widow, it is unjust to penalize the former by deducting life insurance or pension plan benefits from her award. To do so undermines the uniformity and egalitarianism at the heart of the new program.

Of course, this approach would not be problem free.

Why compensate at all?

Whatever the award amount, it would, by definition, have a different impact on different families. A payment of $250,000 would mean much more to the widow of a young soldier with three kids than to the widow of a wealthy stockbroker living in a $3 million home with two cars in the family garage. The same $250,000 award would be more important to a surviving family with no life insurance than to a family with $5 million in insurance proceeds safely deposited in the bank. But differences are not necessarily inequities. The realities of life do not automatically translate into injustice.

Under this approach, it is essential to understand the nature of public compensation. It should be viewed as an expression of the collective cohesive spirit of the nation and its citizens toward the victims of a foreign terrorist attack here at home. It is a recognition of the emotional suffering of surviving families, regardless of economic wherewithal and financial circumstances. In this sense, the economic impact of the award is almost irrelevant; the fact that the award is authorized by Congress at all is what matters. The rest is window dressing, expensive window dressing to be sure, but window dressing nonetheless.

So what should be the amount of the award offered to rich and poor alike? There's the rub. Any amount fixed by Congress undoubtedly will be viewed as arbitrary and unsatisfactory. And if Congress attempts simultaneously to impact other public policies—such as restricting or prohibiting lawsuits—a whole new range of issues and

KF never decides "how much?" -

how much?
↓

problems will come into play. If the flat amount is too little, it will be difficult for Congress to justify restricting or eliminating access to the civil justice system. There is also a looming practical problem: If the government's offer is too little, the high-end families would probably choose to take their chances in the uncertain world of litigation. If Congress is going to minimize the size of awards, it would be wise to leave the courthouse doors open for anybody who wants to sue. Current laws that provide fixed statutory amounts, such as the Public Safety Officers Statute, pay victims' families "only" $250,000, but they do not limit the right to sue. The payment is made as a generous expression of public citizen thanks to police officers and firefighters killed in the line of duty—not as an attempt to limit litigation.

And if Congress provided a modest award and simultaneously barred access to the courtroom, would the law stand up in court? Unlikely. Relatively modest workers' compensation statutes in virtually all states do prohibit the right to sue. But such statutes have the force of history and experience behind them, and provide a compensation program for future work-related injuries. Here, to the contrary, there is the 9/11 fund precedent with its lucrative awards for terrorist attacks that have already occurred. It would be hard for elected officials to justify following the workers' compensation model in light of this glaring example of public generosity.

Or Congress could authorize much larger payments as consideration for prohibiting all lawsuits. This is unrealistic. Congress would probably never pass a law specifically authorizing payments of $2 million to all claimants. The amount is simply too large to pass political muster.

Finally, Congress could take a complete pass and delegate the issue of victim compensation to a special master. Although this might sound like an easy out, it would be unwise and probably unconstitutional—an obvious attempt by Congress to avoid check-writing responsibility. The new special master would also bear the brunt, as I did, of family and public outrage if awards were perceived as too high or too low, becoming the target of every self-appointed guardian of the United States Treasury. That isn't fair or practical.

I've indicated why I think the 9/11 fund should not be used as a precedent for any future compensation program. Does this mean I think that the fund, as well as the law that created it, was a mistake?

No. The statute that created the 9/11 compensation fund can be defended as a unique response to an unprecedented event. In its magnitude and horror, and in its impact on the collective psyche of the nation, 9/11 surpassed the Oklahoma City bombing, the first World Trade Center attack, the bombing of the USS *Cole*, and other comparable tragedies. The 9/11 attacks occurred on American soil, in the heart of our biggest city, and at the headquarters of our military establishment. They did not occur in far-off lands, in an attack aimed strictly at government facilities, or on a navy vessel anchored thousands of miles from home. Nor were they committed by one of our own, a twisted American malcontent. Instead, they were a direct attack by foreigners aimed at the American people themselves. And in the magnitude of the death and destruction they caused, they dwarfed all previous terrorist attacks.

As a result, the 9/11 attacks changed the way we look at ourselves. They have shaken our self-confidence and the way we look at the rest of the world.

In this sense—the scarring of the American character—the 9/11 attacks stand alongside a small handful of historical events: the American Civil War, Pearl Harbor, and the assassination of President Kennedy. We will remember September 11, 2001, as we do December 7, 1941, and November 22, 1963, as horrible and tragic days that galvanized the nation, compelled us to reflect on our own mortality, and demanded that we respond as one people in a collective demonstration of united national purpose.

Following 9/11, the American people rallied around the victims and their families, determined to help. There was an immense outpouring of private charitable giving. And there was the creation of the 9/11 fund. These responses revealed a noble side of the American character. Sympathy for the underdog, sensitivity to the needs of the suffering, acknowledgment of life's vulnerabilities—these factors loomed large in the creation of the fund. We've exhibited this better side of our nature throughout our history, whether helping the victims of illness, famine, or natural disaster, or providing a Marshall Plan to create a new Europe out of the rubble of World War II.

Ironically, the success of the 9/11 fund is largely attributable to its uniqueness. In the wake of those unprecedented attacks, the 9/11 fund had to be creative and bold in forging a response. That response should not be viewed as a precedent for compensation programs yet to come. Just as we continue to learn lessons from the 9/11 tragedy, so too we have much to learn from the strengths and weaknesses of the 9/11 compensation fund.

My administration of the 9/11 fund provided me first-hand on-the-job training in better understanding the soul of America. Whatever flaws there may be in the collective personality of our nation, the American character includes an overwhelming generosity and degree of compassion unmatched by any other country at any other time. The 9/11 fund was America on stage, engaged in a bravura performance for all the world to see. I witnessed the reaction firsthand, every day, when meeting with undocumented worker families in Manhattan and foreign claimants in London. Their response was the same: "America is giving me $2 million tax free. Why? What's the catch? Will I be deported? Do I have to give up my current citizenship? This must be a trick!"

But there were no tricks, no hidden traps, no adverse consequences. The money was available, a gift from the American people, a type of "vengeful philanthropy" aimed as much at the terrorists as at the recipients. America would not be cowed or defeated by the horror of

9/11. On the contrary, the people of the United States would respond not only with muscle, but also with compassion. This "we'll show the world" attitude helps explain the fund. The nation would show no quarter in pursuing the terrorists in Afghanistan and around the globe; it would also undertake an equally determined effort to rescue the fallen and comfort the grieving. The 9/11 fund was not just about saving the airlines or restricting lawsuits; it was also about the nation speaking with one voice and demonstrating the best of the American character.

Appendix

In December 2004, the Department of Justice published the *Final Report of the Special Master for the September 11th Victim Compensation Fund of 2001*. (This two-volume report is available to the public.) The report describes in great detail the underlying statute and regulations, how the program was implemented and administered, and concludes with some personal observations from the special master. At the conclusion of volume 1 are a series of tables that provide important and pertinent data about the program. Some of these tables are reproduced in this book to help the reader better understand the nature of the fund and its impact on the families, injured victims, and the American people.

CLAIMS FOR DECEASED VICTIMS BY INCIDENT LOCATION

Location	# of Claims	Amount Awarded
World Trade Center -- Building	2,388	$5,083,751,440.29
World Trade Center -- Street	209	$439,185,736.33
Pentagon	114	$172,571,215.31
Flight No. AA11	65	$119,638,023.32
Flight No. UA 175	46	$69,556,753.04
Flight No. AA 77	33	$57,908,226.32
Flight No. UA 93	25	$53,649,607.47
TOTAL	**2,880**	**$5,996,261,002.08**

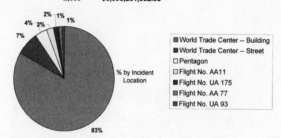

% by Incident Location

- World Trade Center -- Building
- World Trade Center -- Street
- Pentagon
- Flight No. AA11
- Flight No. UA 175
- Flight No. AA 77
- Flight No. UA 93

CLAIMS FOR PHYSICAL INJURY VICTIMS BY INCIDENT LOCATION

Location	# of Claims	Amount Awarded
World Trade Center -- Building	2,212	$892,824,923.59
World Trade Center -- Street/Other	382	$108,687,824.01
Pentagon	86	$51,641,786.96
TOTAL	**2,680**	**$1,053,154,534.56**

% by Incident Location

- World Trade Center -- Building
- World Trade Center -- Street/Other
- Pentagon

CLAIMS FOR DECEASED VICTIMS BY INCOME LEVEL

Income Levels	# of Claims	% of Claims Filed	Total Awards	% of Total Awarded for Death Claims
$0	17	0.59%	$13,396,374.59	0.22%
$24,999 or less	163	5.66%	$179,648,077.33	3.00%
$25,000 to $99,999	1591	55.24%	$2,418,567,253.96	40.34%
$100,000 to $199,999	633	21.98%	$1,457,314,626.24	24.30%
$200,000 to $499,999	310	10.76%	$1,052,333,721.38	17.55%
$500,000 to $999,999	89	3.09%	$422,719,241.32	7.05%
$1,000,000 to $1,999,999	52	1.81%	$294,934,413.48	4.92%
$2,000,000 to $3,999,999	17	0.59%	$106,312,992.16	1.77%
$4,000,000 & over	8	0.28%	$51,034,301.62	0.85%
Total Claims	**2,880**	**100.00%**	**$5,996,261,002.08**	**100.00%**

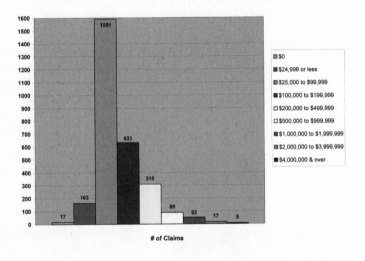

# of Claims

CLAIMS FOR DECEASED VICTIMS
BY GENDER AND AGE

Female		
Age Range	**Claim Count**	**Award Amount**
25 & Under	55	$84,483,690.68
26-30	93	$172,998,972.03
31-40	212	$356,996,222.65
41-50	193	$268,166,342.79
51-60	104	$89,769,339.59
61-70	27	$21,178,460.11
Over 70	8	$5,459,153.75
Sub Totals:	692	$999,052,181.60
Male		
Age Range	**Claim Count**	**Award Amount**
25 & Under	96	$167,352,503.98
26-30	253	$572,081,177.11
31-40	842	$2,347,011,727.86
41-50	630	$1,418,855,991.40
51-60	299	$427,192,091.63
61-70	57	$58,159,862.69
Over 70	11	$6,555,465.81
Sub Totals:	2,188	$4,997,208,820.48
TOTAL	2,880	$5,996,261,002.08

CLAIMS FOR PHYSICAL INJURY VICTIMS
BY GENDER AND AGE

Female

Age Range	Claim Count	Award Amount
25 & Under	14	$2,000,345.22
26-30	28	$14,043,126.00
31-40	137	$45,417,705.00
41-50	135	$55,679,111.21
51-60	87	$16,082,384.00
61-70	13	$1,423,781.00
Over 70	4	$346,933.00
Subtotals:	418	$134,993,385.43

Male

Age Range	Claim Count	Award Amount
25 & Under	26	$3,682,647.00
26-30	117	$58,076,207.00
31-40	776	$387,302,284.72
41-50	988	$374,401,312.97
51-60	307	$87,951,300.44
61-70	43	$6,579,744.00
Over 70	5	$167,653.00
Subtotals:	2,262	$918,161,149.13

| TOTAL | 2,680 | $1,053,154,534.56 |

CLAIMS FOR DECEASED VICTIMS
BY STATE OF RESIDENCE

STATE	NO. OF CLAIMS
Arizona	2
Arkansas	2
California	26
Colorado	2
Connecticut	61
Delaware	2
Districtof Columbia	10
Florida	4
Georgia	2
Illinois	8
Iowa	1
Louisiana	2
Maine	4
Maryland	47
Massachusetts	64
Michigan	2
Misissippi	1
Missouri	2
New Hampshire	9
New Jersey	621
New Mexico	1
New York	1,622
North Carolina	2
Ohio	2
Pennsylvania	29
Rhode Island	5
Tennessee	1
Texas	3
Virginia	94
Subtotal	2,631
Foreign Citizenship/Foreign Residence	249
TOTAL	2,880

CLAIMS FOR PHYSICAL INJURY
BY STATE OF RESIDENCE

STATE	NO. OF CLAIMS
Alabama	1
Arizona	2
California	5
Colorado	1
Connecticut	12
Delaware	2
Districtof Columbia	8
Florida	22
Georgia	2
Kentucky	2
Louisiana	1
Maine	2
Maryland	22
Massachusetts	7
Minnesota	1
Missouri	2
Nevada	1
New Hampshire	1
New Jersey	182
New Mexico	2
New York	2,218
North Carolina	3
Ohio	3
Oklahoma	2
Pennsylvania	24
Rhode Island	3
South Carolina	3
Tennessee	2
Texas	4
Virginia	53
Washington	2
Subtotal	2,595
Foreign Citizenship/Foreign Residence	85
TOTAL	2,680

CLAIMS FOR DECEASED VICTIMS
BY FOREIGN CITIZENSHIP OR FOREIGN RESIDENCY*

Country	No. of Claims	Country	No. of Claims
Argentina	1	Israel	4
Australia	6	Italy	2
Bangladesh	3	Ivory Coast	2
Barbados	1	Jamaica	7
Belarus	1	Japan	23
Belgium	1	Jordan	1
Brazil	3	Kazakstan	1
Canada	18	Lithuania	1
Chile	1	Malaysia	3
China	3	Mexico	5
Colombia	6	Pakistan	1
Dominican Republic	13	Paraguay	1
Ecuador	10	Peru	2
Egypt	1	Philippines	1
El Salvador	2	Poland	2
Ethiopia	2	Romania	1
France	2	Russia	3
Gambia	2	South Africa	1
Germany	8	Sri Lanka	1
Ghana	4	St Vincent	1
Guatemala	1	Sweden	1
Guyana	4	Switzerland	2
Haiti	1	Taiwan	1
Honduras	3	Thailand	1
Hong Kong	1	Togo Africa	1
India	18	Trinidad	3
Indonesia	1	United Kingdom	52
Ireland	2	Ukraine	1
		Uzbekistan	2
		Venezuela	2
		Yugoslavia	1
		Subtotal	249

Citizens of the U.S. with
U.S. Residency 2,631

Total	2,880

*This chart sets forth all death claims where the claimant stated on the claim form that the victim was a foreign citizen or resident of a foreign country. Over 85% of these victims were living in the U.S. on 9/11/01.

CLAIMS FOR PHYSICAL INJURY VICTIMS
BY FOREIGN CITIZENSHIP OR FOREIGN RESIDENCY*

Country	No. of Claims	Country	No. of Claims
Antigua	1	India	6
Argentina	1	Italy	3
Bangladesh	2	Ivory Coast	1
Belize	1	Jamaica	3
Brazil	1	Liberia	2
Canada	13	Kenya	1
China	2	Mexico	1
Colombia	1	Nigeria	5
Cuba	1	Panama	2
Dominican Republic	9	Peru	1
El Salvador	1	Poland	4
France	2	Russia	1
Germany	1	Thailand	2
Ghana	2	Trinidad	2
Guatemala	1	United Kingdom	3
Haiti	3	Ukraine	1
Honduras	3	Venezuela	1
Hong Kong	1		
		Subtotal	85
		Citizens of the U.S. with U.S. Residency	2,595
		Total	2,680

*This chart sets forth physical injury claims where the claim form states that the victim was a foreign citizen or resident of a foreign country. Over 80% of these victims were living in the U.S. when the claim was filed.

GENERAL AWARD STATISTICS FOR ALL CLAIMS

CLAIM DATA FOR ALL CLAIMS			
TOTAL CLAIMS RECEIVED		7,403	
DEATH		2,968	
PHYSICAL INJURY		4,435	
AWARD DETAILS – ALL ELIGIBLE CLAIMS			
TOTAL ALL CLAIMS WITH AWARDS ISSUED			
TRACK A	67% (of awarded claims)	3,735	$3,029,856,022.91
TRACK B	33% (of awarded claims)	1,825	$4,019,559,513.73
TOTAL AWARDS ISSUED		5,560	
TOTAL AMOUNT AWARDED			$7,049,415,536.64
AVERAGE AWARD			$1,267,880.49
MEDIAN AWARD			$855,919.50
MAXIMUM AWARD			$8,597,732.00
MINIMUM AWARD			$500.00
MINIMUM OFFSET			$0.00
MAXIMUM OFFSET			$9,875,656.44
AVERAGE OFFSET			$524,285.58
MEDIAN OFFSET			$236,810.76
TOTAL ECONOMIC & NON-ECONOMIC AWARDS BEFORE OFFSETS			$9,964,443,386.52
TOTAL OFFSETS (ALL CLAIMS)			$2,915,027,849.88
CLAIMS WITH ADVANCE BENEFITS		236	$11,300,000.00
CLAIMANTS RECEIVING STRUCTURES		181	$528,589,421.13

GENERAL AWARD STATISTICS FOR DECEASED VICTIMS

CLAIM DATA FOR DECEASED VICTIMS			
NUMBER OF CLAIMS RECEIVED		2,968	
NUMBER OF CLAIMS DENIED/WITHDRAWN/ABANDONED		88	
TOTAL CLAIMS WITH AWARDS ISSUED		2,880	
AWARD DETAILS – ELIGIBLE DECEASED CLAIMS			
TOTAL ALL CLAIMS WITH AWARDS ISSUED			
TRACK A	47%	1,348	$2,187,641,071.92
TRACK B	55%	1,532	$3,808,619,930.16
TOTAL AWARDS ISSUED		2,880	
TOTAL AMOUNT AWARDED			$5,996,261,002.08
AVERAGE AWARD			$2,082,035.07
MEDIAN AWARD			$1,677,632.54
MAXIMUM AWARD			$7,100,000.00
MINIMUM AWARD			$250,000.00
MINIMUM OFFSET			$0.00
MAXIMUM OFFSET			$9,875,656.44
AVERAGE OFFSET			$855,826.66
MEDIAN OFFSET			$585,657.09
TOTAL ECONOMIC & NON-ECONOMIC AWARDS BEFORE OFFSETS			$8,461,041,778.69
TOTAL OFFSETS (ALL CLAIMS)			$2,464,780.776.61
CLAIMS WITH ADVANCE BENEFITS (216)			$10,800,000.00
CLAIMANTS RECEIVING STRUCTURES (In whole or in part) 178Claims			$519,602,850.13

GENERAL AWARD STATISTICS FOR PHYSICAL INJURY VICTIMS

CLAIM DATA FOR PHYSICAL INJURY VICTIMS			
TOTAL CLAIMS RECEIVED		4,435	
NUMBER OF CLAIMS DENIED/WITHDRAWN/ABANDONED		1,755	
TOTAL CLAIMS WITH AWARDS ISSUED		2,680	
AWARD DETAILS – ELIGIBLE PHYSICAL INJURY CLAIMS			
TOTAL ALL CLAIMS WITH AWARDS ISSUED			
TRACK A	89%	2,387	$842,214,950.99
TRACK B	11%	293	$210,939,583.57
TOTAL AWARDS ISSUED		2,680	
TOTAL AMOUNT AWARDED			$1,053,154,534.56
AVERAGE AWARD			$392,968.11
MEDIAN AWARD			$108,746.50
MAXIMUM AWARD			$8,597,732.00
MINIMUM AWARD			$500.00
MINIMUM OFFSET			$0.00
MAXIMUM OFFSET			$2,972,238.00
AVERAGE OFFSET			$168,002.64
MEDIAN OFFSET			$0.00
TOTAL ECONOMIC & NON-ECONOMIC AWARDS BEFORE OFFSETS			$1,503,401,607.83
TOTAL OFFSETS (ALL CLAIMS)			$450,247,073.27
CLAIMS WITH ADVANCE BENEFITS (20 claims)			$500,000.00
CLAIMANTS RECEIVING STRUCTURES (In whole or in part) 3 Claims			$8,986,571.00

APPENDIX

RECEIPT OF CLAIMS TIMELINE*

Month/Yr. Received	Injury - 4,435	Death 2,968	Total - 7,403
December-01	22	37	59
January-02	69	96	224
February-02	48	54	326
March-02	26	51	403
April-02	27	21	451
May-02	29	27	507
June-02	36	45	588
July-02	30	21	639
August-02	25	29	693
September-02	37	25	755
October-02	16	31	802
November-02	13	38	853
December-02	32	51	936
January-03	35	76	1,047
February-03	29	63	1,139
March-03	316	104	1,559
April-03	103	72	1,734
May-03	24	85	1,843
June-03	25	114	1,982
July-03	89	130	2,201
August-03	31	147	2,379
September-03	155	158	2,692
October-03	235	201	3,128
November-03	337	347	3,812
December-03	2,561	942	7,315
January-04	37	1	7,353
February-04	16	1	7,370
March-04	14	0	7,384
April-04	5	0	7,389
May-04	7	0	7,396
June-04	4	0	7,400
Post June-04	2	1	7,403

* Of 108 claims received after the 12/22/03 deadline, 11 were accepted as timely based on a finding by the Special Master that the Claimant had taken sufficient action prior to the deadline to effect a timely filing. All others were denied.

COSTS ASSOCIATED WITH THE ADMINISTRATION
OF THE SEPTEMBER 11TH VICTIM COMPENSATION FUND

STAFFING & COST ANALYSIS THROUGH SEPTEMBER 30, 2004	NUMBER OF STAFF	ESTIMATED COSTS
I. THE FEINBERG GROUP, LLP -- THE SPECIAL MASTER'S OFFICE	15	$0.00
Kenneth R. Feinberg and the Legal, Administrative and Support Staff of The Feinberg Group worked in excess of 19,000 hours during the period beginning November of 2001 through the present. The value of this time is estimated to be in excess of $7.2 Million.		
Out-of-Pocket Expenses		$ 404,000.00
II. PricewaterhouseCoopers, LLP		
(Including costs paid to subcontractors by PWC)	129 - 474	$ 76,511,000.00
(Total Estimated Costs for PWC reflect actual costs and obligated funds through Fiscal Year 2004)		
III. GOVERNMENT EMPLOYEES ASSIGNED TO THE PROGRAM		
Civil Division Employees (Salaries & Benefits)	13	$ 2,968,000.00
Assistant United States Attorneys	15	$ 636,000.00
Department of Agriculture Detailee	1	$ 63,000.00
IV. ADMINISTRATIVE LAW JUDGES FROM THE FOLLOWING AGENCIES	47	$ 679,000.00
Department of Housing and Urban Development		
Department of Labor		
Environmental Protection Agency		
Federal Energy Regulatory Commission		
Federal Mine Safety & Health Regulatory Commission		
National Labor Relations Board		
Social Security Administration		
United States Coast Guard		
United States International Trade Commission		
V. ASPEN	10 - 50	$ 4,674,000.00
VI. CACI	3 - 10	$ 862,000.00
VII. CONSULTANTS		$ 76,312.00
VIII. PRO BONO ATTORNEYS & HEARING OFFICERS		
2 Pro Bono Attorneys	2	$0.00
4 Pro Bono Hearing Officers	4	$0.00
TOTAL COSTS TO DATE		$ 86,873,312.00

TOTAL COSTS REPRESENT 1.2% OF TOTAL AWARDS

Index

PublicAffairs is a publishing house founded in 1997. It is a tribute to the standards, values, and flair of three persons who have served as mentors to countless reporters, writers, editors, and book people of all kinds, including me.

I. F. STONE, proprietor of *I. F. Stone's Weekly*, combined a commitment to the First Amendment with entrepreneurial zeal and reporting skill and became one of the great independent journalists in American history. At the age of eighty, Izzy published *The Trial of Socrates*, which was a national bestseller. He wrote the book after he taught himself ancient Greek.

BENJAMIN C. BRADLEE was for nearly thirty years the charismatic editorial leader of *The Washington Post*. It was Ben who gave the *Post* the range and courage to pursue such historic issues as Watergate. He supported his reporters with a tenacity that made them fearless and it is no accident that so many became authors of influential, best-selling books.

ROBERT L. BERNSTEIN, the chief executive of Random House for more than a quarter century, guided one of the nation's premier publishing houses. Bob was personally responsible for many books of political dissent and argument that challenged tyranny around the globe. He is also the founder and longtime chair of Human Rights Watch, one of the most respected human rights organizations in the world.

For fifty years, the banner of Public Affairs Press was carried by its owner Morris B. Schnapper, who published Gandhi, Nasser, Toynbee, Truman and about 1,500 other authors. In 1983, Schnapper was described by *The Washington Post* as "a redoubtable gadfly." His legacy will endure in the books to come.

Peter Osnos, *Publisher*